JAPAN'S
Political System

ROBERT E. WARD
University of Michigan

Prentice-Hall, Inc., Englewood Cliffs, New Jersey

COMPARATIVE ASIAN GOVERNMENTS SERIES

Editors
ROBERT E. WARD
ROY C. MACRIDIS

Much of the material in this book
appeared originally in
Modern Political Systems: Asia,
edited by
Robert E. Ward and Roy C. Macridis.

© 1967 BY PRENTICE-HALL, INC.
Englewood Cliffs, New Jersey

Current printing (last digit):
10 9 8 7 6 5 4 3 2 1

Library of Congress Catalog Card No.
67–20230

Printed in the United States of America

PRENTICE-HALL INTERNATIONAL, INC., *London*
PRENTICE-HALL OF AUSTRALIA, PTY. LTD., *Sydney*
PRENTICE-HALL OF CANADA, LTD., *Toronto*
PRENTICE-HALL OF INDIA PRIVATE LTD., *New Delhi*
PRENTICE-HALL OF JAPAN, INC., *Tokyo*

PREFACE

This series is dedicated to the proposition that it is no longer valid or profitable to study comparative politics within an essentially North American- and European-centered frame of reference. Although admittedly more familiar, more comprehensible, and—in the past, at least—closer and more important to us, the political histories, ideologies, and institutions of these areas constitute only a small (though vital) fragment of the political universe with which the student of contemporary political systems must be concerned. Politically speaking, the history of the twentieth century is in large part the history of the re-emergence of non-European areas and states to positions of independence and prominence on the world scene. We can ignore this fact only at our peril.

Asia, Latin America, and Africa together account for approximately sixty-three per cent of the land area and seventy-five per cent of the population of the earth. Today, three factors combine to give new meaning and importance to these figures. First, the age of imperialism and colonialism—at least in the classic sense of these terms—has been largely liquidated. Thus non-Western states—often themselves but recent graduates from colonial status—are obtaining a degree of political independence and freedom of decision and maneuver which is, in a collective sense, unique in their recent histories.

Second, this development is both impelled and accompanied by what is often referred to as "a revolution of rising expectations." Great masses of people in the underdeveloped areas are being exposed to the highly revolutionary concept that meaningful types of economic, political, and social change are possible in their countries, and that these carry with them the promise of a better life for themselves and their children. They are becoming actively dissatisfied with the products and performance of their traditional societies and in increasing numbers are demanding some measure of modernization. It happens that these demands coincide with a period when the skills and technologies necessary to support such modernization are for the first time becoming widely available. Thus most of the governments of these non-Western states—some eagerly, others with trepidation and reluctance—are being committed to more or less systematic long-term efforts to modernize at least segments of their societies. Gradually, therefore, the technological and power gap which has long separated West from non-West is beginning to narrow, and the material circumstances of the two areas are becoming less disparate.

Third, both of the previously mentioned developments are taking place at a time when modern communications and weaponry have made all men uneasy neighbors in a world where global rivalries and ceaseless competition between the "democratic" and "Communist" approaches to political, economic, and social problems have become the predominant international problems. In such circumstances, the political and military weakness of most of these non-Western states is no longer so controlling a factor. In the first place, this weakness is not a fixed condition; some of these states, such as China, have become formidable powers in their own right. In the second place, the very existence of the cold war endows them with an importance and with possibilities of maneuver which they might otherwise lack. No matter how remote their location or "underdeveloped" their circumstances, the territory, resources, skills, and allegiances of each of these states are of significant value in this all-encompassing struggle. From this complex of factors is emerging a world which —even in the conduct of its hostilities—is characterized by new degrees and dimensions of unity and interdependence.

It is essential that the discipline of comparative politics keep abreast of such developments and expand its frames of reference and concern to include the political systems of these emergent non-Western areas. Such a resolution is easy to make, but hard to put into practice. The governments involved are so numerous, their political heritages and institutions so complex and diverse, and the materials and skills relevant to their study and analysis so scattered, uneven in quality, and difficult to use that—for introductory purposes, anyway— we must be highly selective. In the present volume, we direct attention only to the political system of Japan; other books in this series deal in comparable terms with the Chinese People's Republic, India, Southeast Asia, and the Near and Middle East. A further volume treats the political systems of England, France, West Germany, and the U.S.S.R. All were designed in accordance with certain shared views about the nature of modern political systems and the manner in which these may most meaningfully be compared. To make clear the nature of these shared views, we may begin by stating what we believe a political system to be and what factors we hold to be relevant to the comparison of political systems. This will involve the identification of those qualities and problems which we will treat in the case of Japan and of the political systems under consideration in other volumes of the series.

A political system is a mechanism for the identification and posing of problems and the making and administering of decisions in the realm of public affairs, an area which is variously defined by different societies. The official machinery by which these problems and decisions are legally identified, posed, made, and administered is called government. Government provides both an official, authoritative mechanism for the identification and posing of problems and the making and administering of decisions and a means of formalizing and bestowing legitimacy on the products of this process. In practice, it does more than this; by providing a context and an apparatus for the making of official decisions, it also comes to influence the types of problems which are posed and decisions which are taken.

Government—in the sense of society's legislative, executive, judicial, and bureaucratic machinery—is not, however, the sole concern of students of comparative politics; for it is only a part of the political system as a whole, which includes, in addition to government, such informal or unofficial factors as (1) the society's historical heritage and geographic and resource endowments, its social and economic organization, its ideologies and value systems, and its political style; and (2) its party, interest, and leadership structure. Government, plus these two categories of related and mutually affective factors, thus constitutes the political system of a society.

The first step in the analysis of a given political system is to ascertain those aspects of a society's historical, geographical, social, economic, and ideological heritage and endowment—listed under category (1) above—which are significantly related to its political decision-making system. This will provide both a picture of the working environment of a system's politics and an inventory of the basic problems, resources, attitudes, groups, political alignments, and styles of action which relate to its political decision making. For this reason, we refer to such factors in the chapters which follow as "the foundations of politics."

In practice it is not easy to agree, for a given society, on just which of its many characteristics are of present and primary political importance—that is, "foundational"—and which are of only historical or secondary importance. They are not necessarily the same from country to country, nor are they constant for different stages in the history of a single society. Their satisfactory identification and evaluation in any given case is itself a matter which calls for considerable study and sophistication and about which judgments will differ. In general, however, the more unfamiliar, non-Western, and underdeveloped the political system under consideration, the greater the need for explicit and detailed treatment of these foundational aspects of politics. American students simply do not bring to the study of Japanese politics a fund of relevant information or a semi-intuitive "feel" for the situation in any way comparable to that which they bring to the study of their own or some Western European political system. Finally, it should be emphasized that these "foundations of politics," although they are here distinguished from one another, categorized, and treated separately, in fact constitute a unified, national, interrelated, and interactive complex. Their separation here for expository purposes should not lead one to forget this fact.

The interaction between these foundational aspects of a political system and the governmental organs of that system constitute "the dynamics of politics." Social, economic, political, and ideological claims and supports rising from these foundational aspects of a system are constantly being presented to officials and organs of government with the demand that they be converted into public policy. Political parties, interest or pressure groups, and political leaders play the role of conveyor belts between the makers of such claims and the organs of government which make official decisions and establish public policy. They thus serve as active or dynamic agents within a political system, sifting and choosing among the claims which demand action, formulating these in viable terms, gathering support, and presenting the results in the form of demands for political action. These dynamic factors of politics—political parties, interest or pressure groups, and political leaders—thus bridge the intrasystem gap between the political foundations and the formal decision-making organs of government.

The third major component of political systems is government, which is the formal and legitimacy-conferring machinery for the identification and posing of problems and the making and administering of decisions in the realm of public affairs. More specifically, it is the legislative, executive, judicial, and administrative or bureaucratic machinery of state, and the constitutional and legal framework within which these operate. Although distinctive functions and organs of these sorts are usually identifiable in most nonprimitive societies, it should not be assumed that they will be neatly and individually institutionalized along the lines indicated by these traditional categories or that they actually perform the functions indicated. Legislative and executive functions, for example, are often combined, and modern legislatures in practice seldom legislate in the complete, classical sense of that term. It should also be noted that for totalitarian systems such as the U.S.S.R. or the Chinese People's Republic it is largely meaningless to attempt to distinguish beween the governmental roles and powers of the Communist Party and the formal apparatus of state.

In studying any system, we are interested in both the input and the output aspects of its mechanism. Consequently, for a given political system we are interested not only in the previously described "input" process by which it poses, makes, and administers its decisions but also in the nature, quality, and effectiveness of the decisions taken—that is, in the efficiency and performance characteristics of political systems as well as in their mechanics. The "output," or efficiency, of a political system can be gaged by its capacity to survive and by its ability to make decisions that are widely accepted. Assessment of the former is relatively simple. The latter, in a democratic system, can usually be determined by the response which its decisions elicit from social groups, interest groups, and other associations. In a totalitarian system, the test is similar, though the nature of the groups concerned and the manner of ascertaining their responses are different.

An efficient political system maintains a balance between stability and change. Change is an inevitable consequence of the competing political claims that arise among groups as a result of shifting technical, social, and economic conditions and of the demands that such groups press as they struggle to gain positions of influence and power. Efficiency, therefore, is a function of governmental response to such groups and demands. To be efficient, however, such a response must take place within a context of stable and generally accepted political institutions. Otherwise, emerging groups will attempt to gain power by revolutionary means, which have disruptive effects upon the entire system. From this point of view, there is no guarantee that a democratic political system is more efficient than a totalitarian one.

In the chapters that follow, this question of governmental efficiency will be discussed primarily in terms of two aspects of governmental performance. The author is concerned first with matters of relatively short-term performance. How does the Japanese government define its appropriate spheres of political concern and activity? How does it allocate attention, funds, and resources among these spheres of concern? Beyond such relatively specific and short-term issues, however, we are also concerned with certain long-term performance characteristics of political systems. How efficiently has Japan coped with the larger problems of political development and modernization? What forms of political organization and action—democratic, authoritarian, or variants of these—has it found most appropriate to its needs? In whose behalf is the system operating? These are the underlying and enduring problems of all political systems in our time. Their import and urgency will vary within a particular system as well as from system to system, but some combination of these problems is critical for all societies. Together, they provide major themes for all the volumes of this series.

So much, then, for the manner in which we visualize our task. We have defined a political system as a mechanism for the identification and posing of problems and the making and administering of decisions in the realm of public affairs. We have established certain broad categories of analysis for such systems: political foundations, political dynamics, the formal decision-making organs of government on the input side of the process, and governmental efficiency and performance, both short-run and long-run, on the output side. In the chapters that follow, an attempt will be made to apply these categories in such a way as to illuminate the functioning and performance of the Japanese political system.

ROBERT E. WARD
ROY C. MACRIDIS

CONTENTS

Chapter *1*

INTRODUCTION

Less than a hundred years ago, Japan was a little-known kingdom just emerging from a period of self-imposed national isolation that had lasted for almost two and a half centuries. Her territory was restricted to the four main islands of Hokkaido, Honshu, Shikoku, and Kyushu. Her population numbered slightly more than thirty million, some ninety per cent of whom were peasants living in the countryside and working their small farms with tools and techniques differing little from those their ancestors had utilized for the preceding millenium. The national economy, though changing, was still semifeudal in character, while the total impression conveyed by the society has been described by one authority as roughly comparable, in Western terms, to early Tudor times, that is, to the England of more than four hundred years ago.

Politically, the country was, in theory, an empire ruled by an emperor who claimed direct descent, through an unbroken line of illustrious predecessors, from Amaterasu-omikami, the goddess of the sun. In fact, the emperors had long been carefully cloistered in the Imperial City of Kyoto, ritually remote from all meaningful contact with the crude world of politics. Since 1603, Japan had actually been governed by a delicately balanced system, often described as "centralized feudalism," in which prime authority rested with a Shogun, the head of the great House of Tokugawa, who ruled from his family's historic capital of Edo (modern Tokyo).

Politics, like social organization, was carefully stratified along hereditary class lines, and only a small elite was privileged to participate in the making or administering of political decisions. Pre-Restoration Japan was, in short, a species of traditional Asian society: predominantly rural, agrarian, immobile, stratified, authoritarian, and oligarchic in its primary socio-political characteristics. From the Western viewpoint, it was strange and exotic to a degree perhaps most vividly portrayed in the period's favorite art form, the wood-block prints known as *ukiyoe,* which catch so faithfully the style, temper, and appearance of the "floating world" of late Tokugawa times.

When we move forward in Japanese history the space of only one long lifetime, some ninety years from the Restoration of 1868 which overthrew Tokugawa rule, we see an almost miraculously different Japan. During this period, the isolated kingdom had become a great empire, briefly dominating the whole of Eastern Asia, only to lose all its territorial gains in the catastrophic defeat of 1945. Its population, according to the 1965 census, had swollen to upwards of ninety-eight million, a more than threefold increase within a single century, and the majority of the people now dwelt in cities rather than in the country. From small beginnings had sprung a modern industrial and commercial economy which remains the most advanced and productive in all Asia and which, in some respects, rivals or even surpasses those of the United States, the Soviet Union, and Great Britain.

Massive changes in social organization had also taken place: The rigid system of class stratification had been abolished; free, public, and universal education had become the norm; social and economic mobility and opportunities had been greatly enhanced and expanded; equality before the law had been established; and the national standards of living, well-being, and security soared to levels hitherto unknown in either Japan or Asia. Politically, the Emperor remained in Tokyo—rather than in Kyoto—but still as symbol rather than ruler. The Shogun and the old nobility had disappeared and been replaced by a popularly elected National Diet, or Parliament, which operated through a responsible Cabinet. Universal adult suffrage had become the rule, and both national and local government were, to a significant degree, elective and representative. Public affairs were administered by a large, specialized, and professional bureaucracy, and public decision-making systems were predominantly secular, rational, and scientific. Thus change has overtaken Japan at a dizzying rate. When Westerners today visit Tokyo, Osaka, or Kobe for the first time and view the familiar sights of big-city life, they are often inclined to wonder if this can indeed be "the Orient."

We do not have to seek far or delve deep, however, to discover the historic continuities that underlie and, to a large extent, channel the forces of change in modern Japan. Surrounding the Western-appearing cities, for example, lie the fields and villages of Japan, where social, economic, and political changes have been accepted more slowly and in more piecemeal fashion. It is an exaggeration to claim that in reality there are two Japans—urban and modern (or Western) on the one hand, rural and traditional on the other. The facts do not lend themselves to such neat categorizations. But there is enough truth to this proposition to make it both intriguing and challenging. In both cities and villages, the basic and most important unit of social organization continues to be the extended family, followed by the traditional community or some slightly more modern neighborhood or work group. Patterns of social thinking, of decision making, and of conduct are still likely to owe more to these ancient and traditional loyalties or their contemporary analogues than to the insurgent force of individualism. These basic continuities, although less obvious than the changes, are of fundamental importance to any understanding of the over-all course and circumstances of Japan's recent development.

Japan's experience in solving, on the whole successfully, the myriad national, group, and individual problems that beset its attempts to modernize is a subject of vital interest for students of the modern world. In terms of the most meaningful indexes of modernization, Japan stands far in advance of the rest of Asia. It represents what might be termed Asia's sole exemplar of a "mature" society. Most of the other states of non-Soviet Asia—led by Israel, China, India, and Turkey—have only recently begun to perceive and deal systematically, and on their own, with problems and programs that are sixty to ninety years old in Japan. Although the circumstances of these more recent attempts at modernization differ in significant respects from those confronting Japan in the latter part of the last century, such differences should not be permitted to obscure the important degrees of similarity that exist throughout Asia in such spheres as social and economic organization, internal power relationships, status vis-à-vis the West, national aspirations, and selection of national goals and the means to their achievement. Because of such shared factors, Japan's experience foreshadows the experiences and problems of more recently modernizing Asian states and affords useful insights into such general phenomena as modernization, industrialization, authoritarianism, imperialism, and democratization. Indeed, it may be a particularly important exemplar of political modernization. In these times, when we hear so much about the political future of Asia being dependent on the outcome of a competition between the Chinese and the Indian paths to modernization, it should not be forgotten that there is also a Japanese path, which has led the Japanese to considerably more advanced national circumstances than are enjoyed by either the Chinese or the Indians.

Another and more immediate reason why Japan today looms so large in our eyes is the fact that Japan's defeat in 1945 and the Communist victory in China in 1949 fundamentally altered the power situation in Eastern Asia and in the world. Since 1949, the United States has been confronted with expanding responsibilities and commitments in Eastern Asia in the face of greatly increased Communist hostility and strength. Prior to 1945, Imperial Japan effectively checked Soviet Russian influence and ambitions in this area, while a weak and divided China, although generally favorable to the United States, was a negligible power on the international scene. The principal effect of the Allied victory in August, 1945, was to eliminate Japan as a force in Eastern Asia and thereby to enhance greatly the power of the U.S.S.R. in the entire Sino-Japanese area.

With Mao Tse-tung's victory in the Chinese civil war and the rapid consummation of the Sino-Soviet Alliance in February, 1950, Communist influence and strength increased tremendously throughout all Asia, and the United States' position was reciprocally weakened. Since no friendly power was capable of checking Communist ambitions and aggressions in Eastern Asia, the United States itself had to fill the resultant gap. Yet it could not do so effectively without local cooperation. We needed bases in Asia near the frontiers of Sino-Russian power, and we needed Asian friends and allies to contain the spread of the Communists. To some extent, these needs were met through the Southeast Asia Treaty Organization (SEATO), through our various relationships and arrangements with the Philippine Republic, South Vietnam, the Chinese Nationalist Government on Taiwan, and the South Korean Republic, and through the establishment of our postwar base on Okinawa. But all these, although of individual and collective value, still left us in a relatively weak position in—or, rather, off the coast of—Eastern Asia. The advent of growing differences and hostility between the Chinese People's Republic and the U.S.S.R. after 1959 did not materially improve our national circumstances in this respect.

Only Japan in the years 1948–50 had the potential of becoming a formidable bulwark against Communist strength in this Western Pacific area. A decision to ally ourselves with a recent and bitter enemy did not come easily, but the danger was growing rapidly. China, our traditional friend and ally, was lost. Only Japan, our erstwhile enemy, possessed the strategic position, the population, the established economic skills and capacity, the leadership, and the general developmental potential to give us sufficient strength in Eastern Asia. Conversely, it was feared that the defection of this Japanese potential to the Chinese or Soviet causes would almost certainly propel Communist power to ascendancy throughout Asia. Consequently, since 1948–49 the United States has striven to establish relationships with Japan on as firm and friendly a basis as possible.

From a defeated and occupied enemy, Japan has risen in twenty-two years to become our most important and valued ally in Asia. In terms of cold war strategy, her position in Asia bears a close resemblance to that of West Germany in Europe. Like West Germany, Japan's economy and productive capacity are one of the Western alliance's greatest assets. Again, if Germany may be regarded as the western anchor of the chain of Allied military alliances and bases that ring the frontiers of the erstwhile Sino-Soviet Bloc from NATO through CENTO to SEATO and the so-called "island chain" off the coast of Eastern Asia, Japan may be considered the eastern anchor of this somewhat discontinuous and dubious chain of "positions of strength." Against this background, the question of Japan's willingness to continue as our principal military base and diplomatic associate in Asia has assumed international prominence. This and related questions about alternative international arrangements which Japan may prefer have today become major issues in United States foreign policy and world affairs in general. Japan, therefore, occupies a truly critical position in world politics as well as in Asian politics.

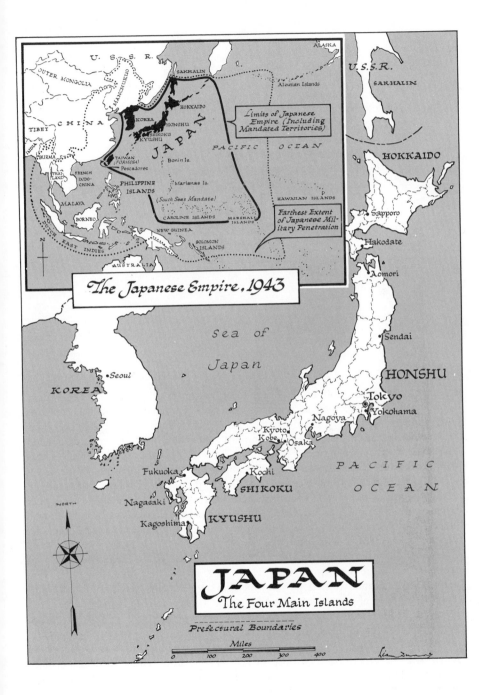

The Japanese Empire, 1943

JAPAN
The Four Main Islands

Prefectural Boundaries

Miles

Chapter 2

The Foundations of Politics

HISTORY

A country's political system is a product of its total culture. Its politics does not develop separately from the geographic, social, economic, ideological, scientific, or historical elements of that culture, but interacts with all of them as both cause and effect. In studying the Japanese political system, therefore, we should first examine its nonpolitical determinants, or what we have referred to as "the foundations of politics." These factors together constitute the larger framework we call "Japanese culture," in which politics is only one element. In the chapters which follow, we shall investigate rather briefly the historical, ecological, social, and ideological foundations of the Japanese political system. The reader is asked to bear in mind, however, that these are artificial divisions and that Japanese society, like any society, is actually a seamless web.

The modern period in Japanese political history dates from the series of events in 1867–68 known as the "Meiji Restoration." At that time, the Emperor Meiji assumed formal power over the state, an act that marked the end of the long rule of the Tokugawa Shogunate (1603–1867). Prior to 1867, the Imperial House had long since abdicated any pretense to actual authority. With very few exceptions, the Emperors of Japan have lacked any appreciable political power since roughly the ninth century A.D. During this long period, Japan was governed by a variety of aristocratic and feudal systems, which, since the latter part of the twelfth century, have normally been controlled by warrior groups. Japan, for much of this time, actually lacked any effective central authority. In 1603, however, after a series of fierce civil wars, Toku-

6

gawa Ieyasu [1] established the ascendancy of his House and imposed on Japan a much greater measure of national government and control (see Table 2-1). By modern standards, it was far from being a centralized government, for some three-fourths of the national territory and considerable political power were still held by more than two hundred and fifty feudal lords known as *daimyo*. But it did constitute the most effective and durable national political system Japan had ever known. It is from the breakdown of this system that the modern Japanese polity proceeds.

TABLE 2-1

BRIEF CHRONOLOGY OF MODERN JAPANESE POLITICAL HISTORY

Date	Event
1603	Beginning of Tokugawa Period.
1867	End of Tokugawa Period.
1867–68	Meiji Restoration and beginning of Meiji Period.
1889–90	Promulgation and enforcement of the Meiji Constitution.
1894–95	Sino-Japanese War.
1904–05	Russo-Japanese War.
1912	End of Meiji Period and beginning of Taisho Period.
1924–32	Period of greatest strength and achievement by prewar Japanese political parties.
1926	End of Taisho Period and beginning of Showa Period.
1931	Outbreak of the Manchurian Incident.
1932–45	Period of growing military ascendancy and ultranationalism in Japanese politics.
1936	Military Revolt of February 26 in Tokyo.
1937	Outbreak of the China Incident.
1941	Outbreak of general warfare in the Pacific (Dec. 7).
1945	War in the Pacific ends (Aug. 15).
	Japan's formal surrender (Sept. 2).
1945–52	Allied Occupation of Japan (Sept. 2, 1945–April 28, 1952).
1946	Promulgation of the new Japanese Constitution (Nov. 3).
1947	Enforcement of the new Japanese Constitution (May 3).
	Beginning of the cold war between U.S. and U.S.S.R.
1950	North Korean invasion of South Korea (June 25).
1951	Treaty of Peace between the U.S. and a majority of the Allied Powers and Japan (Sept. 8).
	Security Treaty between the U.S. and Japan (Sept. 8); revised in 1960.
1952	Allied Occupation ends and Japan regains her sovereign and independent status (April 28).

The Restoration

The events of 1867–68 did not in themselves constitute a revolution, although their long-term consequences were in the deepest sense revolutionary. There was no sustained civil war or insurrection, no massive shift in the basis of political power, no reign of terror, and

[1] Throughout this book, personal names will be given in Japanese fashion, that is, with last names appearing first.

no sudden emergence of a new political or social elite. Still, it was far more than a mere palace revolution. Most of the leaders of the Restoration Movement were members of the privileged military or samurai class, operating with the approval and sometimes the active support of their particular feudal lords and a section of the imperial court nobility. A majority of them came from four of the most remote and powerful fiefs in Tokugawa Japan: Satsuma and Hizen in Kyushu, Choshu in the extreme southwestern section of Honshu, and Tosa in southern Shikoku. They represented primarily these fiefs, not the contemporary samurai class or the anti-Tokugawa elements of the aristocracy as a whole, much less the population of Japan.

The motives of those who opposed the Tokugawa were many and varied. Historic clan enmities against the Tokugawa mingled with the dissatisfactions of the samurai at their deteriorating economic and social status. These feelings were reinforced after 1854 by the threat to Japan's security posed by the consequences of the Perry Treaty, which opened the country to foreign commerce and, it was feared, to Western imperialistic exploitations as well. Much of the blame was attributed, often unjustly, to the Tokugawa Shogunate.

The rebels hoped to legitimize their ambitions by restoring to the Imperial House its rightful position and power, which had long been denied it by the House of Tokugawa and its shogunal predecessors. Their program was, therefore, called the Restoration Movement and its immediate goals were well symbolized by the slogan *Sonno joi* ("Revere the Emperor; expel the barbarians"). Behind such slogans there lay, of course, a variety of more deep-seated and "historic" causes: the widely disruptive effects of the introduction of a monetary system into the old rice-based economy of Tokugawa Japan; the increasing stresses stemming from the commercialization and industrialization of the economy; the very rigidity of the Tokugawa system in the face of cumulative challenges; growing dissatisfaction with the existing class system and relationships; the spread of urbanization and the resulting growth of new social and economic problems; and the development in the Japanese of a sense of nationalism. All these disruptive forces merged in 1867–68 to catalyze the successful movement to overthrow Tokugawa power, and produce the "Meiji Restoration," named after the regnal title of the fifteen-year-old boy who then ascended the throne.

Modern Japanese political history may be said to date from this series of events. The "Restoration" did not mean, however, that the Meiji Emperor was actually "restored" to the powers claimed by his eighth-century ancestors, who were vested by right of divine descent with absolute power over the state. The leaders of the Restoration never seriously considered such a step. In fact, their conception of the Imperial position in government probably did not become definite until the last half of the 1880's, when it was finally embodied in the Constitution of 1889. What did come of the Restoration, however, was the establishment of a new oligarchy, originally military in nature and regional in its political loyalties, with the Satsuma and Choshu clans as primary powers and the Tosa and Hizen fiefs as secondary ones. This new ruling group gradually solidified its control within Japan and launched the country on its difficult and perilous path to modernization. The new oligarchy was led by a truly remarkable group of men: Kido, Saigo, Inoue, Okubo, Iwakura, Ito, Yamagata, Matsukata, and Okuma—a veritable flowering of leadership such as occasionally appears at critical junctures in a nation's history. Although in no sense "democrats," they were able to transcend limitations of background and education and to comprehend the need for a strong and industrialized Japan. Their vision, ability, and strength contributed much to the creation of a new Japan.

The Pre-Constitutional Period, 1868–1889

The twenty-two years that divided the Restoration from the promulgation of the Meiji Constitution in 1889 were years of consolidation and experimentation. The first concern of the new oligarchy was for its own security. Its domestic enemies were many and powerful, and they were not finally overcome until the government's new conscript army put down the great Satsuma Rebellion of 1877. It also continued to fear economic and political intervention by the imperialistic powers of the West. For years, the Meiji oligarchy was preoccupied with plans to strengthen and modernize the country to prevent such intervention. Fear of the West spurred the development of Japanese nationalism and greatly affected the outlook and policies of the new Japan.

Old institutions were uprooted and new ones were introduced at an unsettling rate: the traditional four-class system of samurai, peasant, artisan, and merchant, along with the rights and privileges of the samurai and the Tokugawa fiefs, were abolished, as was the old land-tenure system; in their place came mass public education, conscription, equality before the law, railroads, modern industrial plants, technology, a merchant marine, and a modern army and navy. Politically, the period was marked by experimentation with various forms of government, with no particular one winning out. A professional bureaucracy was established to cope with the expanding needs of the state. A small number of educated Japanese gained their first insight into the political philosophies and systems of the West. Some, led by the Meiji oligarchs, preferred the authoritarian strain in Western thought, perhaps best exemplified at the time by the Prussian state and the dominant Austro-Prussian school of constitutional law. These seemed to the oligarchs to be both more congenial to their native tradition and better suited to the urgent needs of the Japanese state for strong leadership and unchallenged national unity.

Other political leaders, mostly from the ranks of the political dissidents, preferred some version of the liberal tradition in Western thought and studied closely the writings of Mill, Bentham, Locke, Montesquieu, Rousseau, and many others. Members of this "liberal" group organized the first political parties in Japan during the 1870's and launched demands for limited suffrage, more representative government, and a national parliament, to contest the continued dominance of the oligarchs from Satsuma and Choshu. This was a seminal period in Japanese political history, for, although characterized by change and experimentation, it gave birth to both the authoritarian and the liberal traditions which have since constituted the two main streams in Japan's political development. Many of the issues, personalities, and styles of political competition that were to dominate the Japanese political scene for decades clearly emerged during these twenty-two years prior to 1889.

The Meiji Constitution, 1889–1890

The years 1889 and 1890 were years of decision in Japanese history, a political watershed marked by the adoption of the Meiji Constitution, which was promulgated in 1889 and enforced in 1890. This remarkable document served as the legal basis of government in Japan for fifty-five years, until Japan's defeat and occupation in 1945. It was formally superseded only by the present Constitution, which was adopted in 1947. In the Meiji Constitution, the oligarchs incorporated their view that a permanent and modern system of government was needed for effective domestic control and international security. No resuscitated form of the shogunate under Satsuma and Choshu auspices was practicable, although it was considered.

The Constitution also reflected the natural desire of the oligarchs to perpetuate their own authority and that of their selected successors. They justified this provision on the grounds that Japan needed the decisive leadership which only they could supply. Finally, the Constitution adopted those minimal concessions to the doctrine of representative government which its framers judged necessary to placate international public opinion and mounting domestic political opposition. Although scarcely ideal as a foundation for a liberal political system, at least by present-day standards, it should not be forgotten that the Meiji Constitution and governmental system were not notably illiberal in terms of prevailing European practice in 1890. They did mark a major departure from earlier Japanese political institutions and processes.

The Constitution was secretly drafted and ratified and on February 11, 1889, the 2,549th anniversary of the legendary founding of the Japanese state, it was publicly presented to the Japanese people as a token of the Imperial benevolence. The system of government thus established rested on a theory of the state, referred to by the Japanese as *kokutai*. This meant that the Japanese state was intelligible only in terms of its Imperial institution and that, for both theoretical and legal purposes, the Emperor, as the successor of an unbroken line of divinely descended ancestors, embodied the Japanese state. The reigning Emperor, therefore, was the sole ultimate repository of all state powers —executive, administrative, legislative, and judicial. To this authority was added the spiritual authority that derived from his position as a lineal descendant of the sun goddess. He was thus the central figure in the nation's major cult— if not religion—State Shinto. In theory, then, the Meiji Constitution resulted in a system of government that was centralized to a degree unprecedented among the major states of the modern world.

In practice, however, the situation was quite different. Only Meiji, of the three Emperors who reigned under this Constitution, normally played a significant political role. The personal intervention of the present Emperor that brought about the acceptance of the Allied terms and Japan's surrender in 1945 was, as far as we know, unprecedented. The actual power of the sovereign, therefore, was normally not too different from that of most of his pre-Restoration forebears. He lent legitimacy and an aura of sanctity to the political decisions of his ministers and advisers, and simply authenticated their policies through ritualized acts. One should not, however, conclude that the Emperor had no real political significance. On the contrary, since 1868 he has been of basic importance. He provides the Japanese with their sense of historical continuity and serves as their symbol of national identification and as the moral basis and justification for the existence and powers of government. These prerequisites for a stable system of national government did not effectively exist in pre-Restoration Japan, and it is a credit to the Meiji oligarchy's brilliance and leadership that they were able so effectively to use the symbol of the Emperor as a means of unifying the country and building a modern political system.

Power under the Meiji Constitution did not, therefore, reside with the Emperor. In practice, his authority was delegated to a complex array of offices and officials. These delegations were seldom precise or clear-cut, and the resultant system of authority and responsibility was a maze of overlap, duplication, obscurity, and rivalry. Reduced to simplest terms, however, the following were the main elements of the government. The Emperor's executive and administrative authority was divided into military and nonmilitary components. The military component was apportioned to the General Staffs of the Army and Navy for command and operational functions and to Ministers of the Army and of the Navy for administrative functions. Military responsibility was further confused by the establishment of several other military boards and offices with vague and sometimes overlapping functions. The Emperor's nonmilitary authority was delegated largely to a Prime Minister and Cabinet composed of Ministers of State who were in theory responsible to the Emperor.

The national military and civilian authorities were supreme. Local governments had no significant autonomous authority, but functioned under centralized ministerial control. Legislative authority was divided, residing in part in a bicameral legislature and in part in the Cabinet, which could rule by executive order and decree. The Emperor's judicial authority was assigned to a dual system of courts, judicial and administrative, subject to extensive supervision by the Ministry of Justice. The entire government was staffed by professional military and civilian personnel, technically responsible to the Emperor, who were distinctly elitist in training and spirit. In addition, a large staff ministered to the Imperial House and the Emperor himself. This staff often seems to have had a voice in major political decisions.

Even from this brief description, it is apparent that the Meiji Constitution was not intended to establish a democratic political system in Japan. It was frankly conceived by its framers as a means of perpetuating the type of authoritarian rule with which they were personally identified, and this it did with great success for many years. Still, for reasons indicated earlier, it did make certain minimal concessions to popular rights and representative government. These proved to be of greater importance than their drafters anticipated, for they provided the legal and institutional foundations for the subsequent development of political liberalism in Japan.

Among the most important democratic concessions contained in the Constitution were significant grants of civil rights. Although shrewdly hedged about with protective clauses, they did assure Japanese subjects much greater freedom of speech, publication, association, and religious belief than they had ever enjoyed. The most important concession of all, however, was the national parliament or Diet, and its lower House of Representatives in particular. This House was a popularly elected body intended to represent the people of Japan.

It was given qualified powers, shared equally with a conservative and aristocratic House of Peers, to initiate legislation, pass laws, query Ministers of State, levy taxes, and approve the national budget. Through persistent and clever exploitation of these powers, the leaders of Japan's political parties were able, over a period of thirty-odd years, to liberalize appreciably the political institutions inherited from the Meiji oligarchs. But this process of liberalization was slow, difficult, and piecemeal, and, after a brief period of modest ascendancy between 1918 and 1932, it succumbed to the resurgent forces of Japanese authoritarianism.

A prime reason for this failure was the strong authoritarian and antipopular bias systematically built into Japan's basic political institutions by a Constitution that encouraged an elaborate imperial myth and created a powerful but irresponsible cabinet system of government, an equally irresponsible and ultimately more powerful military apparatus, an able but elitist bureaucracy, and no really effective means of coordinating or controlling these disparate elements. The Meiji Constitution provided Japan with a satisfactory and markedly effective government for many years, but it proved fatally inadequate to meet the national needs during the turbulent 1930's and 1940's.

Post-Constitutional Developments, 1890–1932

The time period within which one chooses to analyze a segment of history can greatly affect one's emphasis and conclusions. For example, if we examine only the forty-two-year period of Japanese political history from the enactment of the Meiji Constitution in 1890 to April, 1932, the month before the assassination of Prime Minister Inukai, we could reasonably conclude that Japan's political system was slowly "evolving" along relatively liberal and democratic lines. To be sure, such a judgment would have to lean heavily on the developments of the last eight of these forty-two years, and skirt with caution a number of embarrassing questions posed by the actual quality of so-called "party government" in post-1924 Japan and by the direction and implications of the nation's foreign policies. Such a case, however, could still be made and often has been. Considered in a larger historical perspective, though, it is more accurate to say that Japanese political history during these years was largely a product of two major streams of domestic development: one authoritarian and the other parliamentary and at least proto-liberal. Throughout most of the period, authoritarianism was actually in the ascendancy, and it was to remain so until Japan's defeat in 1945.

Political power was shared during these years among the following major contestants: (1) the Meiji oligarchs and their direct successors in top civilian positions; (2) an increasingly distinct and professionalized group of military leaders; (3) the higher ranks of the civil bureaucracy; (4) leaders of the larger and more important conservative political parties; (5) a big business group usually known as the *zaibatsu;* and (6) an hereditary peerage, many of whom held high posts in the Imperial Court, in the Privy Council, or in the House of Peers. This classification is somewhat arbitrary in view of the many shifts in political roles and allegiances that took place throughout the period, but it does afford a rough framework for analyzing the major developments of the time.

The Meiji oligarchy was, to begin with, largely of samurai background and martial tradition. In the early days, it provided both the civil and military leadership in Japan, and there was little differentiation between the two. It was split along clan rather than functional lines, and such lines were of some importance until as late as the 1920's. During the 1890's, however, the civilian and military wings of this group began to develop along increasingly distinct paths. This was due partially to a natural process of specialization in a rapidly modernizing society, and partially to the Meiji Constitution, which distinguished sharply between civil and military leadership. By 1900, two separate successor groups to the original Meiji leadership had appeared: one primarily civilian, the other military. Although they often disagreed, the gap that separated them on most major issues was usually neither wide nor continuous, and they generally cooperated more than they competed. With time, the connections of both groups with the original Meiji oligarchy declined in importance and, with the deaths of such elder statesmen as Yamagata and Matsukata in the early 1920's, disappeared almost completely. Thereafter, it becomes difficult to distinguish second- and third-generation leaders in these groups from the professionalized bureaucracy.

The social background of Japan's bureaucracy, like that of the Meiji oligarchy, was predominantly samurai and martial. This segment of the population both needed employment as a result of the abolition of its former class status and possessed the educational and administrative skills essential to a modern bureaucracy. As the need for trained civil servants grew, however, more recruits were drawn from the general population and educated at the new state and private universities and technical schools, especially at Tokyo Imperial University. A relatively small, cohesive, and professionally trained higher bureaucracy thus was created. Originally closely affiliated with the Meiji oligarchy, in more recent times it has succeeded to much of its political power.

The career leaders of the major political parties constituted a fourth leadership group. Many of the party presidents came from the ranks of the oligarchs, the bureaucracy, and even the military, but below this level was a large number of party professionals. Although these party leaders were ideologically conservative, they were usually at odds with the civil and military oligarchs and, to a lesser degree, with the higher bureaucracy and the peerage over issues of political position and power. From the 1870's on, the parties demanded a larger role in the decision-making process than was allotted them either before or after the Meiji Constitution. In practice, they continuously attempted to place their members in the premiership and in the nonmilitary Cabinet posts and tried in this fashion to force the Cabinet to recognize its responsibility to the party-controlled lower house of the Imperial Diet. Success in this endeavor would have greatly increased their political power.

The *zaibatsu*, a collective term for the great cartels that controlled a major sector of Japan's economy, also figured prominently, if indirectly, in her politics. Their very size and wealth made it inevitable that they would maintain close association with the government. Their political affiliations varied. All had active bureaucratic connections, and they usually cooperated with both the civilian and the military oligarchy. In fact, they regularly provided sinecure posts for government officials upon their retirement from public service. It was not until after the First World War that some of the largest *zaibatsu* began to ally themselves closely with the major conservative political parties. Political campaigns and elections were very expensive, especially after the introduction of universal male suffrage in 1925, and the *zaibatsu* contributed large sums to campaign funds, which enabled them to exert a substantial amount of political influence.

For our last group of leaders, the hereditary peerage, the most obvious route to power lay through the upper house of the Imperial Diet, which they could control. The House of Peers, however, did not normally play a very positive role in policy determination. As a legislative body in a cabinet-centered governmental system, it suffered from many of the same disadvantages as did the party-controlled lower house. But certain elements of the peerage were active in two other capacities which were of great political significance. The first was the Privy Council, an appointed body charged with advising the Emperor on state affairs, which, from 1890 to the early 1930's, constituted practically a third house of the national legislature. The second agency was the Imperial Household Ministry, which surrounded and served the person of the Emperor. The most important of these men was the Lord Privy Seal. Since he and his associates controlled access to the Emperor and advised him on Japanese and world problems, these officers possessed considerable political power, especially on such critical occasions as the selection of a new Prime Minister.

These six principal leadership groups clashed over many issues in the period 1890–1932, but one in particular merits our attention. This was the continuing struggle by the political parties for greater political power. The Meiji Constitution had carefully restricted the parties to a minor and largely negative role in the governmental process. As the sole formal political spokesmen for the Japanese people, they felt entitled to a much more important and, ultimately, to a dominant role in the decision-making process. They were aided in their struggle by the rising educational standards and political expectations of the Japanese people, by the advance in political participation by certain major sectors of the population, and by the general growth of democratic views and practices in other parts of the world.

But within Japan, those who would have to give up their power to the parties—particularly the civil and military oligarchies, the bureaucracy, and the peerage—were bitterly opposed to any significant expansion of party power. The party leaders, entrenched in their constitutionally sanctioned, if weak, position in the lower house and purporting to speak for "the people," fought back tenaciously and with gradually increasing success. They were able to demonstrate that the Meiji system of government could not operate smoothly or effectively over any considerable period of time without the positive support of a working majority in the House of Representatives. In the most orthodox of Japanese traditions, the party leaders cleverly exploited a position of seeming weakness and eventually achieved a greater share of political power. By 1924, they were beginning to speak of "true parliamentary government" as having almost been achieved in Japan. In fact, the years from 1924 to 1932 are frequently referred to as a "parliamentary" or "democratic" period in Japanese history and was a happy climax to the long struggle between authoritarian and liberal forces that had been launched even earlier than the Meiji Constitution.

Although the slow emergence of a more broadly based system of government through the rise of political parties was certainly one of the most notable developments of the 1890–1932 period, it would be a serious error to regard it as a triumph of "liberalism." The programs and performance of the parties that achieved a brief victory in the late twenties were not very liberal by either American or Japanese standards. Ideologically, these parties were quite conservative. They were much more interested in achieving and exploiting power than in implementing democratic policies, either domestically or in foreign relations. They produced few outstanding leaders and, by neglecting or outraging major sections of Japanese public opinion, they contributed to the authoritarian resurgence of the thirties. Their accomplishments were few, but any other outcome would have been truly remarkable. By 1924, these parties were only thirty-odd years of age, and they had to operate in a society that had been steeped in authoritarian and antidemocratic traditions for many centuries. In those thirty years, they were embroiled in a constant struggle for survival and petty advantages, with little opportunity to broaden their perspectives or acquire a mature sense of public responsibility. Under such circumstances, their shortcomings scarcely appear surprising. The early history of political parties in the West is not notably different.

The Authoritarian Resurgence, 1932–1945

The fourteen-year period from 1932 to 1945 is somewhat embarrassing for those who claim that Japan was gradually evolving into a democratic society. It lasted too long to be shrugged off as merely an episode; it was too dramatic and disastrous in its consequences to be ignored. It marked a reversion to authoritarian and militaristic ways that were certainly far more in the main stream of Japan's political traditions than were the brief years of "liberalism."

The period began with the assassination of Prime Minister Inukai Tsuyoshi on May 15, 1932. This was merely the most conspicuous of a number of such incidents that represented protests against widespread economic—especially agrarian—distress, the corruption and self-seeking of the party politicians during the years of "parliamentary democracy," and a foreign policy held by many to be insufficiently nationalistic or aggressive. These dissatisfactions were exploited by resurgent forces of Japanese militarism and ultranationalism, who felt threatened by the increasing powers of the political parties and the attendant development of a parliamentary system. The militarists and ultranationalists also believed that these were years of unique opportunity for Japan. With intelligence and courage, they held, Japan could become a world power and create an empire that would ultimately dominate all Eastern Asia. But, if this opportunity were missed, Japan would have to resign itself to a slow process of national attrition leading inevitably downward to an insecure and second-class status among the powers.

Since the party and civilian leaders of the day showed few signs of being equal to this challenge, both military and civilian ultranationalist groups in the early 1930's plotted to expel the political parties and replace them by more honest and more aggressive leaders drawn from the ranks of the military or their civilian supporters. The plotters were in disagreement as to both ends and means, but through the years they acquired sufficient force and momentum to bring about great changes in Japanese politics. It is perhaps indicative of the real role of the imperial institution in Japanese politics that they initially cloaked their opposition under the guise of working for a "Showa Restoration," in other words, for returning true "political power" to the Emperor as in the days of the Meiji Restoration—this despite the fact that the present, or Showa, Emperor was apparently opposed quite strongly, although helplessly, to most of what these groups stood for.

During these years, the deterioration of democratic institutions in Japan was steady and rapid—so much so, in fact, that one is inclined to question the extent to which they had really acquired popular support in the preceding period. Domestically, plots and assassinations multiplied, culminating in the famous Young Officers Revolt of February 26, 1936, when some fourteen hundred troops of the First Division seized and held the central districts of Tokyo for three days, while their cohorts attacked seven and assassinated three of the leading statesmen of the day. The principal objects of these attacks—party leaders, big businessmen, and eminent elder statesmen and imperial advisors—tried vainly and ineffectually to salvage what they could from the situation. They sought support from each other, from the Emperor and the Imperial Court, and even, as a last resort, from the military themselves—in short, from everyone except the Japanese people. Ultimately they failed and, after 1936, the military once more determined national policies. The other leadership elements—the bureaucracy, *zaibatsu,* nobility, even the party leaders—were not eliminated from the scene. They simply accepted the inevitability of military ascendancy, compromised with the new circumstances, and formed new combinations and working arrangements.

After 1936, Japan is often said to have become a fascist state. Such a judgment, however, is highly dubious when applied to Japan—at least, if one regards Nazi Germany as the prototype of a fascist society. Many similarities existed, of course, between Germany after 1933 and Japan after 1936. Doctrines of racist mythology, national superiority, and divinely sanctioned imperialism were found in both countries. Both planned to expand into neighboring areas. Between 1937 and 1940, Japan, building upon her earlier acquisitions in Manchuria, pressed forward first in North China, then into the remainder of China, and on down into Southeast Asia in her attempt to establish a nebulously defined Greater East Asia Co-Prosperity Sphere under Japanese guidance and control. This route to empire led in fact to Pearl Harbor, World War II, and finally to defeat and ruin.

Domestically, these were years of growing regimentation, and of expanding governmental control over politics, business, and people's lives in general. In these respects, Japan might possibly have been regarded as a fascist state, but it still differed in a number of important ways from European-style fascism. Nothing in Germany or Italy compared with the imperial institution in Japan. Japan had no *Führer,* no *Duce,* in any way comparable to Hitler or Mussolini. And there was nothing in Japan like the Nazi or Fascist parties. Such "national parties" as the Imperial Rule Assistance Association or the Political Society of Japan were relatively negligible in importance. Japan never really succeeded either in establishing a true dictatorship or in organizing her economy or her politics along truly totalitarian lines. Her experience was thus considerably closer to that of Italy than to that of Germany.

The shattering defeat in 1945 was a stunning blow for Japan, whose modern political history had been composed of little but spectacular successes. The reactions of the Japanese people to this catastrophe varied from class to class, and from individual to individual. Some regretted—and perhaps will strive to recapture—the nation's lost status and power; some welcomed the emancipation from the old order and the expanded opportunities offered by their new circumstances; others, probably a majority, were acutely aware that disaster had struck and that this was not unconnected with the rash policies followed by Japan in the thirties. Thus, although the political consequences of the war and defeat are hard to specify precisely, it does seem probable that the experience significantly increased the people's general involvement in and concern about government and politics. In fact, this is perhaps the greatest political change wrought in Japan by the fourteen years of "authoritarian resurgence."

Prior to the intensification of governmental intervention in economic, social, and political activities following 1937, it had still been possible for many Japanese to live lives that were only lightly or intermittently affected by the national government. This included most of the peasantry and a surprising proportion of urban residents as well. Japan's invasion of China in 1937 and the Second World War brought with them massive conscription, increased taxes, regulation of the labor market and of consumers' expenditures, crop requisitioning, import and export controls, industrial mobilization campaigns, patriotic rallies, and so forth, all of which extended the government's activities deeply into the lives of the people. The greater political awareness and new political interests which resulted have in the postwar years provided a more substantial foundation for the ambitious political reforms of the Occupation era. Such a process of mass "politicization," of course, is bound to have piecemeal and uneven effects, but strangely enough the most durable political consequence of the years of authoritarianism was probably the very considerable heightening of political consciousness and interest that took place at the lower levels of Japanese society.

The Allied Occupation, 1945–1952

At the time of Japan's surrender in August, 1945, the nation was confronted with the awesome costs of the war. Combined military and civilian casualties totaled about 1,800,000 dead; civilians alone accounted for 668,000 killed, wounded, or missing; roughly twenty-five per cent of the national wealth had been destroyed or lost; some forty per cent of the built-up area of the sixty-six major cities subjected to air attacks had been leveled to the ground; about twenty per cent of the nation's residential housing and almost twenty-five per cent of all her buildings were obliterated; thirty per cent of her industrial capacity, eighty per cent of her shipping, and forty-seven per cent of her thermal power-generating capacity were destroyed; forty-six per cent of her prewar territory had been lost, some of it only temporarily, however. Other more intangible costs were harder to calculate: the long-term economic significance of the loss of the Empire; the political consequences of being reduced to the status of a second- or third-class power; the effects of being cut off from established trading partners; the consequences of facing world suspicion and opposition to any revival of Japan's prewar eminence in Eastern Asia. Japan's immediate prospects were ominous and alarming. What was to become of the country? How was it to be reconstructed and rehabilitated?

Many of the immediate problems were taken out of Japanese hands by the Allied Occupation of the country. The Allies formally ruled Japan from the time of the surrender ceremony aboard the *U.S.S. Missouri,* on September 2, 1945, until April 28, 1952, when the Treaty of Peace signed at San Francisco on September 8, 1951 became effective. Japan was required to surrender unconditionally all her armed forces and to accept the arrangements stipulated in the Potsdam Declaration for the establishment of a military Occupation. It was made clear that "The authority of the Emperor and the Japanese Government to rule the state shall be subject to the Supreme Commander for the Allied Powers who will take such steps as he deems proper to effectuate these terms of surrender." At the stroke of a pen, a system of foreign military control was established in Japan that had practically unlimited legal authority to direct all aspects of national life.

In theory this Occupation was an Allied responsibility, but in fact it was an almost exclusively American operation which made a few minor gestures in the direction of Allied participation. The Occupation leaders chose to exercise their authority indirectly rather than directly. Americans did not themselves take over or replace the existing governmental machinery in Japan. Administration continued in Japanese hands, but it was made subject to American direction and supervision. General Douglas MacArthur was appointed Supreme Commander for the Allied Powers (SCAP) to act as the agent in Japan of the victorious powers in general and of the United States in particular. And in September, 1945, an episode began that was unique in modern history—a humane, systematic, and prolonged attempt by a victorious power, vested with plenary legal authority, to remold along more democratic lines the basic political, social, and economic attitudes, institutions, and behavioral patterns of a defeated enemy nation.

The goals and major reform programs of the Occupation were not created out of a void during the fall of 1945. They had been under consideration in the Department of State since at least April, 1942. By the time of the Japanese offer to surrender in early August, 1945, a large number of position papers on the postwar treatment of Japan had been drafted and approved, and by August 29, 1945, a comprehensive statement of the United States Initial Post-Surrender Policy for Japan had been sent to General MacArthur by the State-War-Navy Coordinating Committee. This document established our basic policies toward Japan in considerable detail and, in elaborated form, became a policy directive to General MacArthur by the Joint Chiefs of Staff. In the simplest possible terms, it set forth the two primary objectives of the Occupation:

1. To insure that Japan will not again become a menace to the United States or to the peace and security of the world.
2. To bring about the eventual establishment of a peaceful and responsible government which . . . should conform as closely as may be to principles of democratic self-government but it is not the responsibility of the Allied Powers to impose upon Japan any form of government not supported by the freely expressed will of the people.

In practice, these two goals were commonly called demilitarization and de-militarization.

It is one thing to set such broad and sweeping goals, quite another to achieve them. Demilitarization was a relatively simple problem. It involved arrangements for the surrender and disarmament of the Japanese armed forces at home and abroad, the destruction or conversion to peaceful uses of Japan's arms-making capacity, the repatriation of Japanese military and civilians from all of Eastern and Southeastern Asia, and the complete demobilization and return to civilian life of all members of the armed forces. All these tasks were speedily and efficiently performed by the Occupation authorities. By the end of 1948, Japan had been completely demilitarized, and more than six million soldiers and civilians had been brought home. In addition, a provision was written into Article 9 of the new Constitution that was subsequently to cause much controversy. It renounced war and even denied the nation the right to threaten or use force as a means of settling international disputes. It also seemed to obligate Japan never again to maintain land, sea, or air forces or other war potential. Never before in modern history had a great power been so thoroughly demilitarized.

Democratization was a far more subtle and complicated problem. It raised enormously difficult issues: Whether democracy could be imposed by the orders of a military occupation? What was really meant by "a democratic society"? What aspects of democracy could be successfully transplanted to a society with as different a political tradition and background as Japan? The Occupation authorities did not approach these questions with any very detailed plans for their accomplishment. But, under the pressing needs of the moment, an over-all strategy gradually took form. Essentially, it was based on the proposition that any democratization program would not long survive the end of the Oc-cupation unless sizable and critically placed elements of the Japanese popula-tion were convinced of its value. The basic Occupation strategy, therefore, was to involve a large section of the Japanese people in supporting and im-plementing the reform programs. The Japanese interests that benefited from the major programs are listed on the right below:

Reform Program	*Japanese Interest Served*
1. The purge of ultranationalist officials from designated public and private offices.	Those who succeeded to the offices thus va-cated.
2. Expansion of the franchise.	All adult Japanese women plus all men from 20 to 25 who had earlier been denied the right to vote.
3. The grant to labor of the right to orga-nize and bargain collectively.	Japanese labor in general.
4. Land reform.	The some seventy per cent of farm house-holds that had been tenants or part owners and part tenants before the war.
5. Legal reforms of the traditional family system.	Women and the younger generation in gen-eral.
6. Decentralization of the powers of govern-ment.	Local and regional interests.
7. Educational reforms.	The youth of Japan.

The intent was, first, to create new interest patterns in Japanese society by granting new rights for which there already existed a substantial national demand and, second, to integrate these new interest patterns into a system of interdependent parts. The hope, then, was that each segment of the population that benefited by a particular reform program would, in its anxiety to protect its particular gain, rally to the defense of the entire system when any portion of it was attacked, lest partial revision at any point lead eventually to an assault upon all reforms including their own.

Partially because of this strategy and partially because of a wise recognition of the fact that any viable democratic system must consist of far more than the formal institutions of government, the Occupation approached its task on a very broad front. Political prisoners were set free. Politicians and officials who supported ultranationalism or the old regime were purged from office, and more than two hundred thousand individuals were forbidden to hold public office or certain high managerial positions in private business. The suffrage was expanded to include women as well as men above the age of twenty. New political parties were encouraged. All antidemocratic laws of the old regime were revised. Labor unions were legitimized and encouraged to organize and protect the interests of their rapidly increasing membership. The years of compulsory education were increased from six to nine, and the entire educational system was drastically overhauled, democratized, and decentralized; at the same time, educational opportunities at all levels were greatly expanded. Vast quantities of land were purchased at almost confiscatory prices from absentee, non-tilling, and large landowners and made available to tenant farmers for nominal prices. The highly centralized government of prewar times was radically decentralized, and considerable autonomous power was conferred on the prefectures, cities, towns, and villages. The great prewar cartels, known as *zaibatsu*, were deconcentrated, and their holdings were broken up into independent and competing units. New and unprecedented fair-trade laws and regulations to protect consumer interests were enacted. Public health standards and practices were modernized and improved. New and far-reaching social welfare and social security legislation was devised and enforced. All these and many more "programs of democratic reform" were launched by the Occupation authorities in their broad onslaught on the authoritarian Japanese political tradition.

To anchor these reforms in some durable political form, a new Constitution was adopted on November 3, 1946 (it took effect six months later, on May 3, 1947). This was a most remarkable document. The nature of the political system it established in Japan will be described later in some detail. For the present, it will suffice to note: (1) that it was originally drafted in complete secrecy by Americans on the staff of SCAP's Government Section; (2) that the Japanese government was subsequently persuaded to adopt the American draft under circumstances involving some degree of coercion; (3) that the spirit and institutions of the new Constitution were unmistakably Anglo-American in nature; (4) that the general system of government provided by the Constitution was, technically, among the most democratic in history—for example, it is considerably more democratic than is that provided by the Constitution of the United States; and (5) that the expansive civil rights chapter of the Constitution guaranteed procedural and substantive safeguards that provided basic legal protection for many of the Occupation's democratic reform programs.

The Occupation lasted until April 28, 1952, a total of six years and eight months. Surprisingly, the Japanese were uniformly docile, and frequently friendly and cooperative with their conquerors. It was perhaps the friendliest occupation in recent history. It may also prove to have been one of the most effective. Japanese reactions to particular reform programs varied widely, but the remarkable thing is the extent to which they adopted the majority of them, made them their own, and have continued, even since the end of the Occupation, to support and abide by them. The Occupation's programs in some spheres, however, such as *zaibatsu* deconcentration, many aspects of the local autonomy program, and the decentralization of control over the educational and police systems, have either been abandoned or seriously qualified. But, on balance, it is the Occupation's successful features, rather than its failures, that stand out. The Occupation did bring important political changes and a notable development of democracy to Japan. General MacArthur and his staff deserve great credit for their share in these accomplishments. They served as an essential catalyst at a time when the Japanese people were in a state of unusual flux and receptivity to change, when they were defeated, impoverished, uncertain of the future, desperate for guidance, and lacking in leadership. Once the Occupation had ended, of course, it was primarily up to the Japanese whether they wanted to sustain these changes.

Japan's political history during these years was powerfully affected by developments on the international scene and in the United States. Several factors converged in 1947–48 to produce an important change in the United States' attitude toward Japan. The first was the sweeping and surprising success of the Occupation during its early days. It seemed to most observers that the Japanese had sincerely embraced the cause of reform and were making very promising progress toward a thorough democratization of their society and government. It was also felt that at least a reasonable degree of economic security, with some prospects for future improvement, was essential to the continuance of this democratic progress in Japan. For these reasons and because the Occupation was costly to the American taxpayers, our official attitude toward the rehabilitation of the Japanese economy began to shift decisively during the summer of 1947.

The issue most directly involved was that of reparations: Should Japan be forced to bear a sizable share of the over-all cost of the war through the payment of international reparations and, if so, to whom and in what form should they be paid? Although the American Occupation leaders agreed in principle to the justice of such reparations, it proved impossible to obtain any acceptable international agreement on the scale or method of payment. Any reparations payments that were made seemed ultimately to take place at our expense, since the Occupation had to make good any serious deficits in the Japanese economy in order to maintain viable economic conditions. It was also impossible to induce Japanese enterprise to invest in their own economy as long as they feared that the fruits of their investment could be seized at any time as reparations. In addition, American official circles were increasingly convinced that Japan was no longer a military threat but was, instead, rapidly becoming a peaceable democratic society. Our attitude toward Japan then began to shift from being fundamentally punitive and distrustful to being motivated by the desire to extend assistance toward the political, social, and even the economic rehabilitation of Japan.

Another factor strongly reinforcing this trend was the steady deterioration of the United States' relations with the Soviet Union since the last days of the war. With our decision to provide military and economic aid to Greece in the spring of 1947, the cold war was joined in Europe. At roughly the same time, hope of a negotiated settlement between the Chinese Communists and the Nationalist Government was abandoned, and the civil war in China entered its final stages, presenting the serious threat that a Communist victory in China would extend the cold war to Northeastern Asia. Although this dire event did not actually materialize until the fall of 1949, it affected the United States' view of Japan at a considerably earlier point. If China were lost as an American ally, who could replace her? Obviously Japan was the prime, although an embarrassing, choice. By 1949, we no longer considered Japan as a recently defeated and still potentially dangerous enemy, but as a budding democracy of great promise and an increasingly important, if informal, ally in the cold war.

This shift in attitude directly affected the domestic affairs of Japan. All the basic "reform" programs were conceived and launched in the early stages of the Occupation, when most of the formal orders by SCAP to the Japanese government were promulgated. During these years, SCAP exercised stringent and continuous control over Japanese political and governmental activities. But the year 1948 marked a watershed in the history of the Occupation. After that date, our regulatory efforts steadily slackened and Japanese initiative and activities increased until, for most domestic purposes, Japan again became practically a sovereign power. This was particularly true after General MacArthur was relieved of his post in April, 1951. By the Occupation's end in April, 1952, Japan had, in fact, long since regained her autonomy in many spheres.

In Retrospect

As we look back over the century of Japan's political history since the Restoration (1867–68), two major themes emerge to give some measure of continuity to the confusion of events. The first is the long struggle between the authoritarian, although not totalitarian, tradition and the more liberal groups that stood for some form of constitutional and parliamentary government. The particular issues varied with the times and the contestants, but a constant power struggle was waged between the Meiji oligarchs and their successors and opposition elements, who usually advocated causes considered liberal for the day: a constitution, a parliament, expanded suffrage, Cabinet responsibility, and so forth. Until 1945, the authoritarian forces invariably held the advantage, but the opposition was never eliminated, never totally overcome. It displayed an amazing tenacity and capacity to survive; witness the prompt re-emergence of liberal groups after 1945. Throughout the prewar years, these groups had won few battles, but they did succeed very gradually in altering the basic terms of political competition to their advantage. They obtained a constitution, a parliament, and universal manhood suffrage, and, for a brief time in the late 1920's, seemed on the verge of establishing some degree of Cabinet responsibility and a party system that actually worked. Thus the prewar political history of Japan is not one of unrelieved authoritarian ascendancy, particularly if we compare the Japanese record to that of any other Asian state. There was a gradual, if piecemeal, conditioning of the people in at least some of the basic institutions of a democratic society. In 1945, therefore, Japan entered a period of democratic reform with a considerable heritage of useful political experience.

The second major theme running through Japanese political history is the country's attitude toward Western nations. Since 1854, this attitude tended to swing through cycles of hostility and receptivity. Periods characterized by xenophobia and aggressive nationalism regularly alternated with periods of admiration for and imitation of things foreign and Western. Thus relations with the West, and specifically with the United States, opened on a note of hostility with the Perry missions of 1853–54. This continued through the Restoration of 1868, to be gradually replaced in the 1870's and 1880's by a period of emulation of the West that was often carried to ridiculous lengths. The Russo-Japanese War of 1904–05 marked another high point in nativism and nationalism, which in turn gave way after World War I to a period of *demokurashi* (democracy), when Western ways were all the rage in Japan. The pendulum then swung back to the opposite extreme during the ultranationalist and aggressive days of the 1930's and early 1940's, whereas, since 1945, Japan has displayed new and exceptionally friendly attitudes toward the West and the United States in particular. But, in the light of history, how reliable and how durable are these feelings? Signs of a growing disenchantment with the closeness of Japan's ties to and the degree of her dependency upon the United States have been obvious for some years. In view of these and of Japan's history it is difficult not to speculate on the probability of some degree of progressive disengagement by Japan from the American alliance in the years to come.

Chapter 3

The Foundations of Politics
ECOLOGY

The ability of political systems to create and control the environment in which they exist is limited. As they inherit a particular political history or social structure, so, too, do they inherit a particular set of geographic, economic, and demographic circumstances. These may be alterable, in part at least, by social and scientific planning and controls, but at any given moment in a nation's history, they restrict the range of decisions which that particular political system can realistically make. They thus comprise simultaneously a set of limiting factors of fundamental importance and a set of basic operating resources. Viewed in this light they are among the prime elements which determine the performance of political systems. Let us, then, examine the Japanese endowment in the areas of geography, economics, and population.

Geography

To Americans, the most obvious geographic facts about present-day Japan are that it is small and it is insular. Its total area is 369,662 square kilometers. Compared to the United States (9,-363,389 sq. km.), the U.S.S.R. (22,402,200 sq. km.), or China (9,561,000 sq. km.), this is small. Compared to the United Kingdom (244,030 sq. km.), West Germany (247,973 sq. km.), or France (547,026 sq. km.), it is not. One must beware of American-centered judgments in this respect. In Japan, however, there is an important distinction between the total area of the country and the generally useful or arable land. Only about sixteen per cent of Japanese territory is arable. In terms of this more meaningful index, Japan suffers a great handicap, for the United States has twenty per cent arable land, India has fifty per cent, the United Kingdom thirty per cent, West Germany thirty-four per cent, and France thirty-nine per cent. Among the major states, only the Chinese People's Republic (11 per cent arable land) and the U.S.S.R. (10 per cent) may be in less advantageous positions, although the current accuracy of these percentages is somewhat dubious.

To make matters worse, Japan's national territory has greatly decreased as a result of her defeat in the Second World War. Japan lost Formosa, the Pescadores Islands, Korea, the Kwantung Leased Territory, and the South Seas Mandated Islands—all of which were formerly a part of the Empire (Manchukuo was technically independent). Beyond this, there is little possibility that Southern Sakhalin or the Kuriles will be voluntarily returned by the U.S.S.R., although Japan has not yet formally accepted this loss. Finally, the United States—although acknowledging Japan's "residual sovereignty" over the Ryukyu and the Ogasawara Islands and having announced its intention to return them in the future—continues to occupy and administer both these areas. Japan has thus lost 311,514 square kilometers or forty-six per cent of her total pre-war territory. This amounts to some eighty-four per cent of her present territory. Historically, few states have accommodated themselves readily or with resignation to territorial losses on such a scale.

The bulk of Japan's present territory is accounted for by the four main islands of Hokkaido, Honshu, Shikoku, and Kyushu. There are also more than 3,300 smaller islands within the national boundaries. Japan is a country of islands and mountains, a fact that has profoundly affected the political character of the country. In the first place, it shapes the political unity of the country. Most Americans tend to assume that because Japan is a relatively small state, it is also unified and homogeneous. In fact, this is not so. The islands and the mountains have historically made land communications rather difficult and have produced well-developed patterns of regionality. These regions have traditions and histories of their own and have usually had some sort of political identity as well. In modern political terms, Japan was not really effectively unified until the Restoration (1868), and even today this long history of political decentralization and localism has identifiable political importance and consequences.

Second, the insularity of the country seems to have affected its political history in several significant ways. It has, for example, given to Japan a sharply defined national frontier, so unlike the broad and shifting bands of territory which have historically constituted China's frontiers. This has tended to give to the Japanese a sense of group identity, against outsiders at least, and—when joined with the development of a serious foreign and imperialist threat to their collective security, as was the case after Perry had reopened Japan in 1854—has provided fertile ground for the rapid emergence of strong nationalist feelings. Some would go further and claim that this historic isolation from extensive foreign contacts, made possible by Japan's insular condition, also partly accounts for certain narcissistic qualities in Japanese culture, as well as for the alleged inability of the Japanese to view either themselves or their relations with foreign countries objectively. National isolation may also explain the Japanese tendency to alternate between poles of aggressive self-assertion and a sort of collective inferiority complex in its relation to Westerners and Western culture.

Whatever the merits of such speculations about the Japanese national character, it is certainly true that geography has endowed Japan with a degree of national security that is almost unique in the history of the greater states. It is approximately 130 miles across the Straits of Tsushima to Korea, Japan's closest continental neighbor. It is about 475 miles across the Yellow Sea to the Chinese coast. Japan's safety from invasions from the continent is thus far greater than that of Great Britain, lying 20-odd miles from the shores of France. Prior to 1945, no one had successfully invaded Japan since the ancestors of the present Japanese race did so in prehistoric times. This fact has had two prime consequences for the Japanese. First, it has enabled them to turn on and off almost at will the stream of intercourse with the Asian continent or with the rest of the world. It made possible for example, the effective adoption of a deliberate policy of national seclusion for almost 250 years prior to 1854. Second, it has enabled the Japanese to concentrate exclusively and almost fiercely on domestic political issues, domestic power struggles, and internecine strife, with little or no concern for the effect this might have on the external safety of the nation. National security carried to this extent is unparalleled among the other great states of modern history. It is hard to specify with assurance the consequences of this unique national experience, but the question ought certainly to be posed.

The Economy

In basic resources, Japan is in many respects a poor country. In recent years, she has had to import all her bauxite, all her natural rubber, all her phosphate rock, all her nickel, all her cotton and wool, ninety-eight per cent of her crude petroleum, ninety-five per cent of her iron ore, eighty-five per cent of her copper, and forty-nine per cent of her coking coal. She suffers similar deficiencies in food, although she has in the past few years succeeded in reducing her rice imports to a negligible proportion of total consumption. She continues, however, to import ninety per cent of her sugar needs, eighty-three per cent of her soybeans, eighty-two per cent of her wheat, and thirty-six per cent of her barley.

Against this apparent poverty of resources, however, stand Japan's impressive accomplishments in the general field of economic development (see Appendix, Table II). In 1963, for example, she produced approximately fifty-nine per cent of the electric energy known to have been generated in all of Asia excluding the U.S.S.R., far more than France or Italy and more than West Germany. In the production of crude steel, she ranked fourth in the world, behind the United States, the U.S.S.R., and West Germany. In cement production, she held third place behind only the United States and the U.S.S.R., while in the production of merchant shipping she led the world. These achievements are truly remarkable when one considers the condition of Japanese industry at the end of the war. As early as 1955, in fact, Japan's official indexes of industrial activity, public utilities, industrial production, and manufacturing in general had all broken through their prewar and wartime ceilings, and they have since gone on to unprecedented highs. The gross national product has risen from a postwar low of $3.6 billion in 1947 to upwards of $78 billion in fiscal 1965. During the same period, the nominal national income on a per capita basis rose from $34 to $633. Even when adjusted in light of changes in the general price index, this still means that real national per capita income has more than tripled since 1947. Both production and consumption have risen enormously. As in the case of West Germany, defeat has proven to be but a prelude to the greatest spurt of economic development in recent Japanese history. One is tempted to conclude that, in an economic sense at least, it sometimes pays to lose wars.

The contrast between Japan's poor resource endowment and her flourishing industrialized economy immediately suggests the importance of foreign trade to her economy. Most of the raw materials for Japanese industry must come from abroad. They must be imported in large quantities, processed in Japan, and then either consumed at home or exported to foreign markets to obtain the foreign exchange necessary for the purchase of additional raw materials. The Japanese economy is thus like a throat or funnel into which imports are poured, in which manufacturing and processing take place, and out of which flow finished products for domestic consumption and the export trade. Let us examine this process in somewhat greater detail, first on the import and then on the export side.

In recent years, judged in terms of value, Japan's eleven major imports have normally been crude petroleum, cotton, lumber, wool, iron ore, sugar, scrap iron, petroleum products, coal, nonferrous ore, and soybeans. These account for approximately fifty per cent of the total national imports. They come primarily from the United States, Australia, Canada, Kuwait, the Philippine Islands, West Germany, Malaya, and Saudi Arabia. The United States has been by long odds the most important supplier of Japan's overseas purchases, providing in 1964, for example, twenty-nine per cent of all Japanese imports, at a cost of almost two billion dollars. Japan has for some years been the United States' second best foreign customer, standing behind only Canada in this respect. To meet the cost of these imports, Japan's most important exports have been machinery, iron and steel, ships, cotton fabrics, rayon and synthetic fabrics, clothing, marine products, and radio sets. Such items account jointly for approximately sixty-eight per cent of Japan's total exports. They have been sold primarily to the United States, Hong Kong, Australia, the United Kingdom, the U.S.S.R., the Chinese People's Republic, India, the Philippine Islands, and Liberia (whose purchases consist almost entirely of ships). Again, the United States accounts for a top-heavy proportion of this, taking in 1964 twenty-eight per cent of Japan's total exports, at a price of nearly 1.7 billion dollars.

This flourishing pattern of imports and exports has in postwar times resulted in an adverse balance of visible trade for Japan. Her imports normally exceed her exports by annual amounts ranging in recent years from $436,-000,000 to $1,288,000,000. The fact that Japan usually buys more goods and services from the United States than it sells to this country by no means indicates, however, that Japan makes a net contribution to our international payments position. During the eleven-year period from the end of the Occupa-

TABLE 3-1

JAPAN'S NATIONAL INCOME BY INDUSTRIES AND REAL NATIONAL INCOME [a]   (In billions of yen)

Fiscal year	National income	DOMESTIC NATIONAL INCOME Total	Primary industry Agriculture	Forestry	Fishery	Total	Secondary industry Mining	Construction	Manufacturing	Total
Average 1934–36	14.4	14.4	2.4	0.2	0.2	2.9	0.3	0.5	3.6	4.4
1930	11.7	11.7	1.6	0.2	0.2	2.0	0.2	0.5	2.5	3.1
1935	14.4	14.4	2.4	0.2	0.2	2.8	0.3	0.5	3.7	4.5
1940	31.0	30.9	5.9	1.0	0.6	7.5	0.9	1.0	9.3	11.1
1944	56.9	56.8	7.8	1.3	1.0	10.1	1.4	2.2	19.3	22.9
1946	360.9	360.9	112.3	18.0	9.8	140.1	10.9	24.9	59.3	95.1
1950	3381.5	3383.7	717.3	66.0	96.1	879.4	98.7	136.6	839.5	1074.8
1951	4525.2	4527.7	898.3	111.1	119.0	1128.4	167.6	171.5	1125.6	1464.7
1952	5084.9	5095.9	958.5	123.1	136.1	1217.7	201.8	217.5	1199.6	1618.9
1953	5747.7	5758.7	941.5	160.1	165.0	1266.6	170.6	273.0	1395.9	1839.5
1954	6022.4	6050.9	1008.0	154.3	161.9	1324.2	150.8	294.0	1427.7	1872.5
1955	6718.9	6744.2	1202.2	146.9	181.4	1530.5	135.0	334.0	1565.4	2034.4
1956	7627.6	7659.9	1088.1	172.9	192.8	1453.8	178.5	387.3	2011.9	2577.7
1957	8285.9	8324.6	1131.2	200.7	204.5	1536.4	212.2	420.7	2225.8	2858.7
1958	8519.0	8554.1	1158.4	188.1	218.3	1564.8	192.4	468.9	2209.1	2870.4
1959	10048.8	10087.2	1222.4	195.7	242.2	1660.3	193.2	567.3	2827.2	3587.7
1960	11999.7	12054.7	1338.0	243.8	271.5	1853.3	204.5	739.2	3629.0	4572.7
1961	14213.8	14280.0	1399.1	321.6	321.4	2042.1	227.2	936.7	4395.7	5559.6
1962	15746.9	15829.3	1580.9	283.4	355.7	2220.0	235.7	1079.0	4774.9	6089.6
1963	18265.5	18368.0	1678.6	314.4	383.5	2376.5	242.6	1301.6	5882.7	7126.9
1964	20522.5	20656.1	1832.2	332.9	427.2	2592.3	249.2	1564.6	6341.5	8155.3

TABLE 3-1

JAPAN'S NATIONAL INCOME BY INDUSTRIES AND REAL NATIONAL INCOME (Continued)

DOMESTIC NATIONAL INCOME (cont.)

Fiscal year	Tertiary industry							Net income from abroad	Real national income					
	Wholesale and retail trade	Finance, insurance, and real estate	Transportation, communications, and other public utilities	Services	Other unclassifiable	Government service	Total		National income by distributive shares A	Total population (in thousands) B	Nominal national income per capita (yen) $C=\frac{A}{B}$	General price index D	Real national income $E=\frac{A}{D}$	Real national income per capita (yen)[b] $F=\frac{C}{D}$
Average 1934–36	2.0	1.5	1.5	1.5	0.2	0.5	7.1	−0.0	14.4	68,647	210	1.00	14.4	210
1930	1.8	1.3	1.6	1.4	0.1	0.4	6.6	−0.0	11.7	63,872	183	0.97	12.1	189
1935	2.0	1.5	1.5	1.5	0.2	0.5	7.1	−0.0	14.4	68,662	210	1.01	14.3	208
1940	3.7	2.1	2.7	2.6	0.4	0.8	12.4	0.1	31.0	71,400	434	1.97	15.7	220
1944	3.9	3.0	5.1	3.9	0.3	7.6	23.7	0.2	56.9	73,800	771	3.79	15.0	203
1946	38.5	9.1	15.8	56.0 (Services + Other unclassifiable)		6.3	125.7	—	360.9	75,325	4791	48.8	7.4	98
1950	559.5	109.0	250.1		510.9		1429.5	−2.2	3381.5	83,167	40,659	237.9	14.2	171
1951	792.0	145.9	330.7		660.0		1934.6	−2.5	4525.2	84,475	53,569	273.4	16.6	196
1952	832.0	217.5	413.1		796.7		2259.3	−11.0	5084.9	85,750	59,299	284.6	17.9	208
1953	912.3	300.5	494.3		945.5		2652.6	−11.1	5747.7	86,983	66,078	309.5	18.6	213
1954	962.6	310.7	546.5		1034.4		2854.2	−28.5	6022.4	88,220	68,266	323.3	18.6	211
1955	1064.8	371.5	628.2		1114.8		3179.3	−25.3	6718.9	89,233	75,296	321.9	20.9	234
1956	1234.3	459.2	712.4		1222.5		3628.4	−32.3	7627.6	90,122	84,636	326.1	23.4	260
1957	1301.6	552.0	821.0		1284.9		3929.5	−38.7	8285.9	90,887	91,167	333.7	24.8	273
1958	1333.6	595.7	861.3		1328.3		4118.9	−35.1	8519.0	91,725	92,875	332.7	25.6	279
1959	1604.0	756.6	1014.8		1463.8		4839.2	−38.4	10048.8	92,592	108,528	338.5	29.7	321
1960	1916.4	886.6	1172.8		1652.9		5628.7	−55.0	11999.7	93,383	128,500	348.9	34.4	368
1961	2252.2	1022.9	1437.5		1965.7		6678.3	−66.2	14213.8	94,240	150,826	371.1	39.9	406
1962	2443.8	1206.2	1596.3		2273.4		7519.7	−82.4	15746.9	95,133	165,525	394.2	40.0	420
1963	2930.0	1416.2	1848.2		2670.2		8864.6	−102.5	18265.5	96,110	190,048	419.1	43.6	453
1964	3295.6	1521.1	2022.8		3069.0		9908.5	−133.6	20522.5	97,135	211,278	440.2	46.6	480

a *Nihon Tōkei Nenkan*, 1965.
b In 1934–36 yen.

29

tion in 1952 through 1962, for example, the United States paid to Japan more than six billion dollars, largely in the form of U.S. military expenditures in Japan and secondarily through the offshore procurement in Japan by the United States of economic goods and services intended for third countries. Prior to 1959 there were also small amounts of direct U.S. economic aid to Japan. Net capital flows from this country to Japan added another billion dollars to Japan's holdings of U.S. capital. When these outflows are balanced against Japan's deficits on her merchandise trading and services account with the United States, Japan emerges with a net balance-of-payments advantage of more than $1,500,000,000 for this 1952–62 period. In recent years, however, the size of U.S. military expenditures and of offshore aid procurement in Japan has been steadily decreasing. It declined from a high point of $795,000,-000 in 1953 to $387,000,000 in 1962 and is continuing to decline.

Still, this combination of an unfavorable visible trade balance and dependence on American sources to offset it has created special and unusually important economic relationships between Japan and the United States. Japan would undoubtedly prefer to reduce the extent of this dependence on American policy and the American economy, but under present circumstances it is most difficult to find a satisfactory alternative.

The Japanese economy is thus heavily dependent on foreign trade. Still, it is by no means unique among major states in the degree of this dependence. If we express degrees of dependence in terms of the percentage of gross national product accounted for by foreign trade, we will find that in recent years West Germany, France, Great Britain, and most of the other countries of Asia have all been more dependent on foreign trade than has Japan (Appendix, Table VI). Nevertheless, the survival of the Japanese economy is heavily dependent on foreign trade, and the global conditions and decisions affecting the volume and terms of that trade are largely beyond Japan's sphere of control. Any marked decrease in the global volume of foreign trade is almost certain to affect economic conditions in Japan rapidly. Since 1950, the Japanese economy has become increasingly prosperous, but this should not obscure the fact that the stability of the Japanese economy is notably vulnerable to external pressures and influence. At present, this vulnerability is most pronounced vis-à-vis the United States, but before too long the Chinese People's Republic and the U.S.S.R., singly or jointly, may be in a position to bring appreciable economic pressure to bear upon Japan. The postwar Japanese economy has not yet been faced with a serious test of this sort nor by the sort of unplanned test represented by a prolonged depression. It is by no means easy to foresee either the economic or the political consequences of such an experience.

Population

The 1965 census population of Japan was 98,281,955 (Table 3-2), about three times the national population of 1870 and just double the population of 1910. Japan thus has the seventh largest population of any modern state—ranking behind China, India, the U.S.S.R., the United States, Indonesia, and Pakistan. The population distribution is 265 people per square kilometer of present national territory, or—a somewhat more

TABLE 3-2

INCREASE IN JAPAN'S POPULATION, 1920–1965 [a]

| Year | Population | INCREASE OVER PRECEDING CENSUS OR ESTIMATE | |
		Number	Percentage
1920	55,391,481	. . . .	. . . . .
1925	59,179,200	3,787,719	6.8%
1930	63,872,496	4,693,296	7.9
1935	68,661,654	4,789,158	7.5
1940	72,539,729	3,878,075	5.6
1945	71,998,104	−541,625	−0.7
1950	83,199,637	11,201,533	15.6
1955	89,275,529	6,975,892	7.3
1960	93,418,501	4,142,972	4.6
1961 [b]	94,285,000	866,499	0.93 [c]
1962 [b]	95,178,000	893,000	0.95 [c]
1963 [b]	96,156,000	1,078,000	1.03 [c]
1964 [b]	97,190,000	1,034,000	1.07 [c]
1965	98,281,955	4,863,454	5.2

[a] Adapted from *1965 Population Census of Japan: Preliminary Count of Household and Population,* and *Nihon Tōkei Nenkan, 1965.*
[b] Estimate in mid-censal period.
[c] Percentage increase over preceding year, rather than over the preceding five years.

meaningful figure—1,621 per square kilometer of arable land, the highest density among the major nations. Male members of this population had, in 1964, a life expectancy at birth of 67.7 years and females had an expectancy of 72.9 years, figures which compare quite favorably to our own.

The postwar population history of Japan is unique. Immediately after the war, as a result of the demobilization of the armed forces and the repatriation to Japan of some six million Japanese soldiers and civilians resident in other parts of Asia, the national birth rate per thousand of population soared to 34.3, a figure very close to the 1920's record high of 36.3. Thereafter, it declined steadily to 17.6 per thousand in 1964, one of the world's lowest rates and well below the United States figure of 21.7. Along with this rapid decline in the birth rate has been an equally impressive decrease in the death rate per thousand—it dropped from 14.6 to 6.9 per thousand between 1947 and 1964, largely owing to improved medical services and a national health insurance program. Again, this death rate is appreciably better than the 9 to 12 per thousand recently characteristic of the United States, Great Britain, France, and West Germany. The result of such developments has been a sharp decline in the rate of natural annual increase of the Japanese population, from a postwar high of 21.6 per thousand in 1948 to 10.7 by 1964. Thus a population which was increasing by such fantastic annual increments as 4.99 and 3.10 per cent in the 1946–47 period of repatriation has in recent years been increasing only at a rate of about one per cent or less per year (Table

3-2). The official projections indicate that small increases may continue until the population peaks at some 105 million about 1990, after which it might decline.

So abrupt a decline in national rates of natural increase is unprecedented in modern demographic experience. It was due in the first instance to the economic hardships of early postwar days plus the enactment in 1948 of a Eugenics Protection Law which legalized abortion and made it readily and cheaply available to persons desirous of limiting the sizes of their families. In a number of recent years there have been more than one million registered abortions in Japan. If one adds to these the sizable number of unregistered abortions, the resulting figure may well come close to or surpass the total number of live births occurring annually in Japan. Since 1952, the increasing popularity of contraception as a means of limiting family size has reinforced this effect of abortion on the declining birth rate.

With these developments, the basic nature of Japan's population problem has been changing in recent years, and the nature of the political and economic problems which it poses have changed accordingly. The difficulties associated with a rapid increase of population with no end in sight are being brought under control. They have been replaced, however, by the new problem of a population weighted toward the working ages (15 to 60), a segment of the total population which is now increasing at twice the prewar rate. Japan needs approximately one million new jobs per year to meet this demand. It is anticipated that this type of pressure will remain acute until about 1970, when the nation will begin to confront the quite different economic and political questions presented by a large and increasing portion of the population aged sixty or more. This will greatly inflate the present need for social welfare, old-age insurance, and so on. Massive changes such as these in population balance and characteristics pose basic problems about the management of Japan's economy. They also help define the underlying issues of politics and determine in important measure the general content and style of the political power struggle.

Chapter *4*

The Foundations of Politics
SOCIAL STRUCTURE

Any government or political system inherits and has to work with a population possessed of certain basic social characteristics. Its people may be analyzed and described in terms of prevailing social and class structure, social and political mobility, ethnic and religious composition, income distribution, literacy and education, generational differences, urban-rural distribution, and a great variety of other important categories. The particular configurations which these assume in a society at any given time are closely linked to and help define the power structure and the terms of political competition within that society. Of equal importance, they also delineate a large part of the fundamental problems which a political system must face and solve. Let us look briefly at contemporary Japan in these terms.

Ethnic Characteristics

Japan has a remarkably homogeneous population. Although hybrid in their historic origins, the latest available statistics indicate that of a total population of 97,190,000 in 1964, only 659,789 (0.7 per cent) belonged to registered minority groups. Of this number, 578,545 (88 per cent) were Koreans, 49,174 (7 per cent) Chinese, and 15,626 (2 per cent) Americans. The figures for all other nationalities were insignificant. Although these figures exclude foreigners who have assumed Japanese citizenship, there is no other major nation with so small an admixture of identifiable minority elements. This helps to explain the strong nationalism frequently displayed by the Japanese in modern times. Their geographical isolation, common language, and long history combine with racial identity to facilitate the development of a very strong "in-group" feeling against foreigners. The result is a nation which, although subject to a number of domestic cleavages, has in the past usually presented a strong and united front to the rest of the world.

Sectionalism

We must distinguish, however, between Japan's outward-facing and inward-facing character. Racial homogeneity and nationalism have not precluded the development of a rather pronounced political, cultural, and economic sectionalism. We must not forget how close to the present Japan's pre-modern past lies. The Restoration occurred just a hundred years ago. Most of her national history before that was more local than nation-centered. Geography conspired with feudalism and the limitations of pre-modern communications to insure such a result. The Restoration itself was originally a conspiracy centering about four principal southwestern clans, which is to say, about specific regions or sections of the country. Until well into the present century, the new system of government established by the Meiji oligarchy was denounced by its opponents as clan-dominated. Sectionalism has thus played a continuous and important role in Japanese political history. Today, sectionalism is still important to an understanding of Japanese politics but in a somewhat different guise. Clan affiliations are largely forgotten, but domestic differences in language, culture, tradition, and economic characteristics and interests reinforce the distinctly regional quality of most politicians' sources of political support in a way which enhances the role of sectionalism in the political process. As politicians grow more responsive to local interests and pressures, the importance of such sectional considerations may increase rather than diminish.

Urban-Rural Distribution and Employment Characteristics

Throughout much of Asia, the distinction between city-dwelling and country-dwelling is of fundamental importance. Asian societies are predominantly agrarian, and most of the people are farmers living and working in the countryside. Cities, although by no means new, usually account for but minor proportions of the total population. Yet as the modernizing process takes hold in these countries, the urban sector of the population steadily grows in size and changes its social characteristics. Industrialization occurs first in the cities; migrants flow in from the surrounding countryside; foreigners and foreign ideas gain a foothold and old ways and old social relationships begin to break down; in short, the city becomes the vanguard of the change from a traditionally organized to a modernizing society, whereas the countryside—less directly subject to many of the forces of change—tends to cling more closely to the established and traditional ways.

This process has political as well as economic and social consequences. In Japan, for example, the urban population has definitely been more receptive to political innovation than has the rural population. Liberalism, socialism, Communism, the local autonomy movement, and many other new political movements have been primarily identified with the urban population.

The urban portion of the Japanese population has steadily increased. When the first really modern census was taken in 1920, only 18.1 per cent of Japan's total population lived in cities (Table 4-1). By 1930, this figure had increased to 24.1 per cent, by 1940 to 37.9 per cent, by 1960 to 63.6 per cent, and, according to the most recent census of 1965, to 68.1 per cent. To be sure, the Japanese statistic-gathering system somewhat overstates the truly urban segment of the population, but, even so, it is still true that in forty-five years the distribution pattern has altered from one in which more than four-fifths of the population dwelt in the countryside to one in which well over half live in cities.

These figures are generally confirmed by an analysis of the occupational characteristics of the Japanese working class (Appendix, Table II). The 1963 statistics, for example, indicate that only 28.9 per cent of the total labor force of 46,130,000 was employed in the primary or typically rural industries (agriculture, forestry, and fishing). Of the remainder, 30.5 per cent was employed in the secondary industries (mining, construction, and manufacturing), while another 39.7 per cent was in tertiary industries (trade, finance, communications, government, services, etc.). Thus, in 1963, 70.2 per cent of Japan's total labor force was engaged in the more modern secondary and tertiary sectors of industry. This is quite a contrast from conditions in 1920, when some fifty-four per cent of the Japanese labor force was still employed in agriculture, forestry, and fishing. Basic changes of this sort in employment characteristics and urban-rural distribution mark a profound change in the socio-political qualities and potentialities of the Japanese people.

Income Distribution

The economic characteristics of a nation's population vitally affect the country's political attitudes and behavior. Economic dissatisfaction is conducive to political dissatisfaction which may, under appropriate circumstances, lead to political instabilty and change. In the case of Japan, there can be no doubt that the country's remarkable prosperity in recent years has had a great deal to do with the stability of its political system. Should these economic circumstances change markedly for the worse, corresponding political changes would undoubtedly follow, although it is difficult to foresee their specific nature.

The gross facts of income distribution in Japan are as follows. National income has risen steadily and sharply during the postwar years (Table 3-1). From 1,961.6 billion yen, in 1948, for example, it had climbed by 1963 to 18,265.5 billion yen, an increase of 927 per cent in fifteen years. The most recent figure available is 20,522.5 billion yen (a 1,041 per cent increase) for fiscal 1964. Not all of this represents a real increase, however, since it was accompanied by some measure of inflation, but if we compensate for this by

TABLE 4-1

URBAN-RURAL POPULATION DISTRIBUTION [a]

Census year	POPULATION			PERCENTAGE		AREA IN SQUARE KILOMETERS			POPULATION PER SQUARE KILOMETER	
	Total	All cities	All rural	All cities	All rural	Total	All cities	All rural	All cities	All rural
1920	55,391,481	10,020,038	45,371,443	18.1	81.9	379,420.77	1,367.80	378,052.97	7,326	120
1925	59,179,200	12,821,625	46,357,575	21.7	78.3	379,422.79	2,173.94	377,248.85	5,898	123
1930	63,872,496	15,363,646	48,508,850	24.1	75.9	379,878.62	2,943.09	376,935.53	5,220	129
1935	68,661,654	22,581,794	46,079,860	32.9	67.1	380,159.18	5,086.97	375,072.21	4,439	123
1940	72,539,729	27,494,237	45,045,492	37.9	62.1	380,159.18	8,844.45	371,314.73	3,109	121
1945	71,998,104	20,022,333	51,975,771	27.8	72.2	368,451.43	14,520.07	353,931.36	1,379	147
1947	78,101,473	25,857,739	52,243,734	33.1	66.9	368,469.86	15,894.42	352,575.44	1,627	148
1950	83,199,637	31,203,191	51,996,466	37.5	62.5	368,284.15	19,815.28	348,326.69	1,575	149
1955	89,275,529	50,288,026	38,987,503	56.3	43.7	369,660.74	67,761.23	300,598.95	742	130
1955 (readjusted) [b]	89,295,529	50,288,026	38,987,503	60.8	39.2					
[c]	—	43,261,685	—	48.5	—					
[d]	—	10,992,014	—	12.3	—					
1960	93,418,501	59,333,171	34,084,057	63.5	36.5	369,660.74	82,559.42	285,654.98	719	119
[c]	—	48,291,072	—	51.7	—					
[d]	—	11,042,099	—	11.8	—					
1965	98,281,955	66,925,735	31,356,220	68.1	31.9					

[a] Derived from *1960 Population Census of Japan*, Vol. I, *Nihon Tōkei Nenkan, 1965*, and *1965 Population Census of Japan: Preliminary Count*.
[b] Indicates the 1955 population of all cities and all rural areas according to the boundaries as of 10/1/60.
[c] Indicates the population of all cities having 50,000 inhabitants or more and its ratio to the total.
[d] Indicates the population of all cities having less than 50,000 inhabitants and its ratio to the total.

including changes in the general price index, we find that real national income increased 467 per cent by 1963. Even on a per capita basis, real national income increased about 407 per cent from 1948 to 1963 and far exceeded its prewar high. National income per capita for 1964 was 211,278 yen ($587), and by 1965 it had risen to 227,880 yen ($633).

These steady rises in national and per capita income figures have been accompanied by real improvements in the average standards of living in both the cities and the countryside. Spending for consumer goods has increased markedly, especially in such "nonessential" categories as increased education, recreation, and luxury or semiluxury purchases, including refrigerators, washing machines, and television sets—often humorously referred to in Japan, as "the three national treasures" of the 1960's. Beyond this, the Japanese people as a whole benefit from the vastly expanded welfare and social security programs which constitute so important a part of recent national budgets. The government now provides several types of public assistance and social insurance programs, spends a good deal of money for child welfare programs, and operates both a national health insurance plan and several medical treatment plans. These programs, although new and still far less than adequate for the national needs, represent a notable social improvement achieved in a very short space of time.

A number of serious inequities in the distribution of this unaccustomed national prosperity exist in postwar Japan, for not all parts of the population share equally in these improvements. This is particularly true of that large sector of the economy which the Japanese refer to as "small and medium industries." These are in part still seriously depressed. In this and other sectors, much remains to be done to improve average living circumstances, but on balance the remarkable fact has been the tremendous improvements in standards of living which recent years have brought to Japan. Measured against Japan's previous experience, this has truly been a time of "the greatest prosperity since the emperor Jimmu," that is, since the legendary foundation of the empire in 660 B.C.

Literacy and Mass Media

Japan is one of the world's most literate nations. Three to four years of elementary education were required for all Japanese children as early as 1886. In 1908, this was increased to six years, and, since 1947, nine years of combined elementary and junior secondary education have been compulsory. Practically universal literacy (97–98 per cent) and a very respectable minimum level of modern elementary education are, therefore, the rule. In addition, Japan has one of the most modern and complete systems of secondary and higher education to be found anywhere in the world (Appendix, Table III). In 1964, for example, there were 4,028 senior secondary schools, with a total enrollment of 4,634,408 students; 339 junior colleges with an enrollment of 127,904; and 291 colleges and universities with a total of 852,572 students. About one out of twelve Japanese in the 18–21 age group was regularly enrolled in a college or university, a very high national figure by any but American standards.

Japan's consumption of the mass media is correspondingly high (Appendix, Table III). In 1962, for example, the Japanese were purchasing 420 daily newspapers per 1,000 of population—a figure considerably in excess of our own figure of 311—and in 1960 they published some 27,387 separate titles of new books and reprints—a figure substantially in excess of that for the United States. They also produced more feature-length films than any other country in the world. Practically every household had a radio, and three in every four households had a television set. Japan is literally saturated by the outpourings of the mass media, most of which devote a considerable amount of space or time to subjects directly or indirectly related to politics. Under such circumstances, it is difficult to sustain the Western stereotype of the average Asian as both politically ill-informed and apathetic. Whatever his political views and behavior, the average Japanese is exposed to a very substantial amount of political information and stimulation, even by the most advanced Western standards.

Generational Differences

A deep rift has opened between the political attitudes and behavior of the older and younger generations in Japan. Since adequate research is lacking on this subject, it is difficult to say with any precision just where the boundaries should be drawn and what the dimensions of this split are. But there is general agreement that members of the wartime and postwar generations—roughly children born since 1937—are considerably more apt to have socialist or Communist political views and allegiances than are their elders. Estimates vary with the commentator and the particular youth group under consideration. One study claims that forty-one per cent of the 20–24-year-old age group voted in favor of left-wing—or, as they are called in Japan, "progressive"—political programs and parties in the 1958 general election. Others say that a majority of the new voters coming of age every year vote socialist or Communist at their first opportunity. This tendency seems to have moderated in recent years, however. A poll taken after the 1963 general election, for example, showed only thirty-two per cent of the 20–24 year olds voting for socialist candidates.

It is quite obvious that two organizations that reflect the political views and activities of many students are themselves rather rigidly and militantly Marxist —*Zengakuren* (the National Federation of Student Self-Government Associations) and *Nikkyoso* (the Japan Teachers' Union). Many college and university students, although a small minority of their age group, are among the most vocal, active, and, occasionally, violent supporters of left-wing causes. The political sympathies of other elements of the youth group—such as rural as opposed to urban youth, or high school as opposed to college students, or workers as opposed to students in general—are less certain. But polls do indicate that the "progressive" parties and candidates have the support of a disproportionately high segment of the younger voters, especially among the student and urban youth contingents, whereas a top-heavy proportion of the older voters are of "conservative" political allegiances.

The reasons for this phenomenon are debatable. Some observers note that political interests and activities—often radical or revolutionary in nature—are a part of the student tradition in Asia. Some simply say that radical political views are characteristic of youth in most modern societies, especially in disturbed postwar or cold war times. Others attribute this radicalism to the influence of the allegedly unsettling and ill-advised changes in the national school system introduced by the American Occupation, in combination with the radical sympathies and indoctrination of many of the present teachers. The major question, however, is this: With maturing years, will most Japanese youth retain or discard their left-wing political loyalties? Again, the evidence is inconclusive, but there is increasing reason to believe that a large number become more conservative as they grow older, and change their voting habits accordingly. Were this not so, socialism would be sweeping Japan. Recent election results, however, do not confirm such a trend.

Religious Affiliations

For most Japanese, religious attitudes and persuasions do not seem to have an appreciable effect on their political attitudes or behavior. This is a rather surprising development because of the political uses to which prewar Shinto was put, because of the seeming importance of organized religion in postwar Japan, and because many Westerners expect a people's religious affiliations to affect their politics. The symbols of religion are everywhere in Japan—temples, shrines, priests, and pilgrims—and the average Japanese is a registered member of some faith. In fact, he is usually a member of two faiths —the Buddhist and the Shinto—at the same time (only a bit more than one-half of one per cent of the population is Christian). But this dual allegiance normally carries with it rather modest doctrinal and spiritual commitments. Religious considerations do not seem to bulk large in the average person's decision making, particularly where political decisions are concerned.

There are, of course, exceptions to this generalization. The political militancy of national Shintoism before the war, with its systematic emphasis on the divine descent of the Emperor, on Japan's world mission, and on the citizen's duty to be unquestioningly loyal and obedient, is found today in a scattering of small right-wing bands. And a few of the so-called "new religions" do have strong political views or programs which they strive to impart to their followers. The *Sokagakkai,* is the most notable of these. It claims a membership of more than fifteen million and has organized a political party (the *Komeito*) that is currently the third largest in the House of Councillors and the fourth largest in the House of Representatives. It is an exception to the general rule, however, where organized religions and politics are concerned.

Class Structure and Mobility

Despite all the attempts to analyze Japanese society in Marxist or class-oriented terms, it is still impossible to describe the structure of this society on the basis of its social classes with any accuracy. In Japan as elsewhere, we lack satisfactory definitions of precisely what is meant by such terms as upper, middle, and lower classes—or their many variants—and we do not have enough information to determine what proportions of the population should be assigned to which classes. We can, therefore, discuss the class structure of Japanese society only in a very broad way.

Whatever may be its precise characteristics, present Japanese class structure is the product of a series of quite unusual historical forces. To begin with, a century ago Japanese society was very rigidly stratified into a four-class hierarchy, ranging from the samurai, or warrior class, at the top through the peasantry and artisans to the merchants at the bottom. Although this ranking frequently did not accord with the actual distribution of wealth or influence in late Tokugawa times, it did represent a very important aspect of the status and value system of the time. It was legally abolished only after the Restoration of 1868. Then came the social and economic tumult of early and mid-Meiji years (roughly 1868–1900), which brought with it very considerable changes in class structure.

A new form of hereditary aristocracy was established in 1885. Numerous elements of the old samurai class were ruined, both financially and socially, through their inability to adjust to the new economic circumstances; many others sought refuge in business, the bureaucracy, or the new armed forces and managed to survive in the upper strata. In the countryside, a new sort of status system based on a variety of landlord-and-tenant or -laborer relationships began to emerge, while in the cities there was a comparable ferment among the artisan and merchant classes. Out of this period of pronounced social flux and mobility gradually came a new and more modern system of class relationships. Important elements of the old pre-Restoration class system remained, but new avenues of upward social mobility appeared—through commerce, industry, the bureaucracy, political parties, or the armed forces. Noble or samurai descent, however, continued to be of appreciable social importance. By the 1930's, this new system had pretty well jelled.

Then came the Second World War and Japan's defeat and occupation. This brought with it another great period of social change which is still in process. At the upper levels of society, the hereditary aristocracy and the military elite were eliminated from positions of leadership. The big business element was shaken up. Many political leaders were purged from politics, at least temporarily. Only the bureaucracy remained largely immune from the most drastic aspects of this great reconstitution of Japan's political elite. At lower social levels, even more massive and important changes have taken place. Before the war, the Japanese middle class was, by Western standards, small in both numbers and socio-political importance. Since the war, it has expanded enormously in both size and importance. In the cities, this development has resulted from the postwar growth and diversification of Japanese industry, commerce, and government, the improved status and welfare of employees in general, and the economy's great prosperity since 1952. In the countryside, it has been the product of land reform, technical improvements, and unprecedented prosperity. As the middle class has expanded, the lower class has diminished. It now constitutes a much smaller proportion of the total population than was the case before the war.

Precise information is lacking, but income statistics, consumers' purchases, the results of polls, biographical data, and a variety of other indicators testify that recent years have witnessed an almost unprecedented amount of upward social mobility in Japan. The specific political consequences of this social surge forward are rather hard to identify, however. Class by itself does not, in Japan, provide a very satisfactory explanation of popular political attitudes or behavior. Major segments of the population are not particularly class conscious politically. Conservative political allegiances are by no means based primarily or exclusively on "the middle class," nor are radical allegiances very closely correlated with "lower-class" or "proletarian" status. Given the general trend of recent developments, one wonders, furthermore, whether class consciousness is apt to become a major political determinant. It doubtless could be a significant factor in Japanese politics, and, if a major depression or other disaster were to befall Japan, it might become a crucial one. For the present, however, we must look elsewhere for the key to a fuller and more adequate understanding of Japanese politics.

Chapter 5

The Foundations of Politics
IDEOLOGY

Politics also has its psychological dimensions. Ultimately, what men do politically is determined by what they think and feel and by their apprehension of what is desirable, what is feasible, and what is safe for themselves, their families, and their communities. The political decisions involved are sometimes reached rationally and consciously, but usually they seem for most people to be based on a combination of reason and a broad range of half-perceived or dimly intuited assumptions about authority, government, politics, the state, and the nature of the good society. These beliefs and assumptions, whether explicitly held or vaguely apprehended, constitute the ideological foundations of a political system. They differ remarkably from society to society and from time to time. Their appeal, their authority, and the extent of their acceptance have a potent effect on the stability and the effectiveness of the political system concerned. Such qualities as patriotism, self-discipline, and a sense of public interest spring from such ideological sources. Collectively, and without pejorative intent, we often find ourselves referring to these basic beliefs and assumptions as the political myths of a society.

In modern times, the political myths of a society seldom command universal allegiance. They change, and the attitudes of people toward them also change. At any given moment, some portion of the population is apt to dissent more or less strongly from any particular proposition generally held by the population. This is definitely true of postwar Japan. Before its defeat, the nation was far more unified in support of its myths than it is today. The major watershed in this respect was the year 1945. Defeat, the American Occupation, and the over-all course of postwar liberalization and democratization have discredited many of the prewar myths in whole or in part. In many ways, Japan is today a nation in search of new and more satisfactory political myths. This complicates our problem, for it is hard to tell which myths are now obsolete, which are on the way out, and which will probably retain viability and appeal for substantial segments of the Japanese people. The present situation, therefore, is unclear and can only be described in mixed and qualified terms.

Legitimacy

Under this heading, we are concerned with a variety of fundamental questions. First, how do the Japanese view their form of government from the standpoint of its legitimacy? Does its authority over them seem to be based on some right and proper title, or is it simply a result of the government's control of such instruments of mass coercion as the police and the armed forces? The mass of the population, now as before the war, does not seem to entertain serious doubts or reservations on this score. The average Japanese seems to conceive of government in general, including his own, as part of the fundamental order of things, as natural indeed as the family system, after which the earlier Japanese political system was systematically modeled in both Tokugawa and post-Restoration times. This is quite a different basis for legitimacy than the theories of social contract or general will encountered in the West, but it seems reasonably efficacious in Japan. The basic assent on the part of the Japanese people to their form of government, however, is no longer as general as it was before the war, when the entire conception was more closely identified with the "divinity" of the Emperor. Today, for example, the legitimacy of the government is challenged by dissident Marxists, by those who regard the present form of government as imposed upon a helpless Japanese people by the American Occupation, and by those on the extreme Right who advocate a return to imperial rule in Japan. But at present, these are minority elements and sentiments.

The Emperor

We are also concerned with those mythical or symbolic elements in Japanese culture which affect the political solidarity of the Japanese people. Apart from the fluctuating issues and controversies of current politics, what basic attitudes and assumptions on the part of the Japanese people make for national political unity or consensus? What attitudes produce conflict and dissension? One of the factors that increases national cohesion, as we have already mentioned, is the insular nature of Japan, which gives the Japanese a common identity and unites them against all outsiders, all non-Japanese. To this must be added the role of the Emperor and the Imperial Family as a unifying symbol.

Before 1945, the official myth, systematically contrived in early Meiji times from bits and pieces of ancient Japanese history and rigorously instilled into the people by all possible means, was that the Emperor was descended in direct and unbroken line from Amaterasu-omikami, the pre-eminent goddess of the sun, and that rule over Japan was divinely entrusted to him through his ancestors. Under these circumstances, the Emperor was—in crude translation— "divine," or, as the Japanese say, he was a *kami*. A more appropriate modern rendering would be that he was a superior and awe-inspiring personage of more than natural attributes. The official interpretation proceeded from this basis to state in vague and deliberately mystic and mystifying language that the Emperor was somehow fused with the Japanese "state," that the two concepts could not, in fact or theory, be disentangled from one another—they mutually informed and gave meaning and substance to each other. Somehow, the Emperor was the "state" and, as such, was a "divinely" descended, all-powerful, sacred, inviolable, and absolutely sovereign figure. This was the basic theory of the state in post-Restoration Japan, known officially as the doctrine of *kokutai* or "the national polity." It was also the basis for numerous assertions, official and otherwise, that the Japanese were a unique and superior race with a "divine" mission to spread the blessings of their culture to lesser breeds of men, especially in Eastern Asia.

To us, this entire belief is apt to appear spurious, fantastic, and quite incomprehensible on rational grounds, but in fact it is little if any more nonsensical than other political myths that have commanded the impassioned support of millions of dedicated followers within the twentieth century. How well do the mythical bases of Italian Fascism, German Naziism, Russian Communism, or, in a different genre, the social contract aspects of democratic theory withstand rigorous logical analysis? In any event, this interpretation seems to have been either believed or accepted by a substantial majority of Japanese before the war, and, as a consequence, the Emperor became the basic symbol of the legitimacy and the unity of the state. The public authority was wielded in his name and with his sanction, governmental acts were construed to be manifestations of his will, and the loyalty and patriotism of most of the people were fiercely and sincerely focused on his person—all this, despite the fact that in practice the Emperor actually possessed very little political power and usually had but limited influence on the formulation or execution of public policy.

Since Japan's defeat and the enactment of a new Constitution in 1946, the legal and theoretical position of the Emperor has been drastically changed, although his actual power remains negligible. Early in 1946, he formally and publicly renounced any claims to divinity or superhuman status which might have been made on his behalf. The new Constitution carried this further by stripping him of all vestiges of sovereign power and political authority of any sort; it specifically declared him to be no more than "the symbol of the State and of the unity of the people, deriving his position from the will of the people, with whom resides sovereign power." Thus the prewar position of the Emperor has been completely inverted. Despite this, he remains the single most powerful symbol of the political identity and unity of the Japanese people. He is a different sort of symbol to be sure—less awesome, more human and democratized —but he is still the focus of most popular political loyalties, although these too seem to be considerably less ardent and demonstrative than before the war. There are also more people who challenge the imperial institution. Many younger Japanese and numerous intellectuals abstractly favor the abolition of the monarchy, charging that it is outdated, anachronistic, and useless. Until, however, it can be replaced in the minds and hearts of most Japanese by some other equally strong symbol of their unity and nationhood, it would be dangerous to eliminate the Emperor.

Nationalism

Another basic factor contributing to the political solidarity of the Japanese people is their nationalism. Prior to 1945, the ardency and aggressiveness of Japanese nationalism had long been one of the most conspicuous features of Japanese culture. It has provided the strongest sort of mass support for both the domestic and foreign programs of the Japanese government and, in particular, for the series of generally profitable overseas campaigns and wars that began with the Sino-Japanese War of 1894–95 and culminated disastrously with the Second World War. Defeat and postwar developments in general have worked strange changes in the quality of Japanese nationalism, however. What was a strong flame now seems to be but a dim and flickering light. Prewar martial and aggressive qualities seem to have been replaced by a general spirit of pacificism, internationalism, and an absorption with commercial and peaceful pursuits.

Some observers—including many Japanese—conclude, therefore, that Japanese nationalism is a dead or dying force or that it is in the process of being replaced by a new spirit of internationalism. But such a judgment seems premature. Japan's national circumstances since the war have been markedly peculiar and, in general, not of a type conducive to the re-emergence of Japanese nationalism. To begin with, there were the massive facts of defeat, devastation, and national collapse, both economic and spiritual. This was attended by about seven years of American military occupation, followed by a period of very close attachment to the American side in international affairs. These were also years during which Japan was a constitutionally disarmed nation, supporting only the weakest and scantiest of military establishments masquerading under the name of "self-defense forces." During this postwar period, Japan had not really played a prime or prominent role on the international scene or in the cold war. In foreign policy, she has operated along only limited lines and from an unusually protected and secure position on the fringes of the Western camp—somewhat similar to that of West Germany in Europe.

This sheltered or removed quality, plus a widespread and sincere desire to avoid becoming involved in any military or diplomatic arrangements that could lead to war, has convinced many Japanese that no real threat to their national security exists at present. It is perhaps this feeling that accounts for the present quiescence of Japanese nationalism. Nationalist sentiments often flourish only against a background of some real or apprehended threat to the national security or ambitions. Most Japanese today have no overseas ambitions of the prewar sort and many—unrealistically, we might say—see no real threat from abroad. If these circumstances change, however, as they probably will, it is quite likely that we will witness a re-emergence of some more conspicuous form of Japanese nationalism. It seems highly doubtful that nationalism has ceased to exist as a basic unifying force in Japanese politics; rather, it is merely quiescent.

Monism

Some peoples conceive of government as a supreme and exclusive form of social organization whose power and authority should, when legally exercised, override and control almost all competing claims. Such governments in modern times are apt to play a very positive and extensive role in their societies. Others think of government as one among a number of social organizations—such as the family, the church, and a variety of economic, professional, and cultural organizations—possessed of a unique and, for some purposes, superior type of power and authority but with no right to control or perform all social functions within its boundaries. Governments so conceived tend to play a more restricted role in their societies and to leave many major functions largely to other social organizations. For our purposes, we shall call the first a monist and the second a pluralist view of government and its functions. The Japanese have typically adopted a monist view.

The concept of either individual or institutional rights as in any way removed from or immune to governmental control is completely alien to the Japanese tradition. No real or meaningful sphere of private decision or action was legally or theoretically recognized in Japan until the enforcement of the present Constitution in 1947. It was generally assumed that government could do whatever in fact it had the power and the inclination to do. This right was qualified on occasion by authoritative statements as to how a virtuous ruler or government should deport itself, but these were often of more theoretical than practical consequence. Since 1947, the law has changed in this respect, but public consciousness in general would still seem to lag considerably behind. Changes are occurring as particular minorities are moved to challenge the government's authority and interpretations on such controversial matters as rearmament, foreign policy, and so forth, but it is still probably fair to say that most Japanese accept and usually endorse a very wide range of governmental action and control. The seeming prominence of private enterprise in Japan, therefore, is decidedly misleading. The government is heavily involved in a great variety of ways in what seem to be private operations in the economic and social spheres.

Political Participation

In making an ideological analysis of a people, we should also know how they regard acts of political participation. Are such acts considered the exclusive prerogative of a particular social class, or does the average man regard himself as having some significant rights of participation in the political decision-making process? Again, where Japan is concerned, the verdict must be mixed. The Japanese traditionally have looked upon politics as an activity reserved to the upper classes. In post-Restoration times, this restriction was somewhat abated by the grant of a very limited and sterilized suffrage in 1890 and by its subsequent expansions. It was not until 1925, however, that universal manhood suffrage was introduced and, even this, owing to the very limited authority of the elective lower house of the National Parliament, did not really mark the advent of effective popular participation in politics. Particularly in the case of the peasantry, there seems to have been little effective assimilation of the concept of the vote as a means of participating in and controlling major public decisions. Government continued to seem to be something which was done to such people by their superiors, rather than something done in any part by themselves. It is hard to accustom a people to the idea of effective political participation when they have for so long regarded politics as the exclusive domain of their superiors.

Since 1945, women, too, have been given the vote, and new and more meaningful forms of popular political participation have been established. Still, some of the prewar difficulties persist, especially in the countryside and among certain segments of the urban population. Most Japanese basically do not regard government as in any sense the servant of the people. Consequently, it is difficult for them to accept and act effectively on the Western conception of informed and responsible individual political participation as the fundamental means of asserting and enforcing their collective mastery.

Egalitarianism

The popular Japanese conception of equality is closely related to their view of political participation. Are men generally regarded as political equals, possessed of basically the same rights and responsibilities, or are some regarded as superior or more privileged than others? The answer is complex. Traditionally, of course, Japan had an unequal, or elitist, society. Relatively few people, all in the upper classes, had any political rights. Under these circumstances, political equality was a concept which simply did not occur to the Japanese. There was nothing in their experience and apparently little in their aspirations to sustain such a notion. After the Restoration, however, the idea of political equality was borrowed from Western writings by some of the early party leaders and political thinkers, but it was usually applied in a highly restrictive fashion to members of the "better" classes only. Gradually, however, the concept of equal political rights was expanded until today all adult Japanese subjects have substantially equal political and legal rights. This particular type of equality has, therefore, been established in Japan.

But, in political attitudes and behavior, numerous vestiges of traditional elitism still survive. There is still a strong tendency among large segments of the population—particularly among farmers and the poorer and less-educated urban classes—to regard politics as beyond their proper sphere of concern. Their inclination is to look to someone more sophisticated and experienced than they are for advice on political decisions of all sorts. As a consequence, the political boss, often in the form of a respected local figure whose political advice is widely followed, is a very common phenomenon in Japan. Such individuals, in effect, control very sizable elements of the Japanese electorate on a highly personalized basis. This practice, of course, seriously detracts from the real significance of the equality which is legally guaranteed to all electors.

Another type of political inequality is also prevalent in Japan. It concerns the individual's relationships with and attitudes toward government and government officials. Since the Japanese generally do not regard government as the servant of the people and since Japan did not experience anything comparable to the American or French Revolutions in her history, most Japanese assume that both the government and government officials have superior status and rights. This feeling is fully shared by the great bulk of the officials themselves. The concept of bureaucrats as "public servants" has small reality in Japan for either the average citizen or the bureaucrats. The background, training, and spirit of the bureaucracy is normally elitist. As a consequence, a citizen usually approaches the government diffidently, not assertively. This fact also diminishes the possibilities of a meaningful egalitarianism in Japan.

"Personalism"

There are two major types of political allegiance: programmatic or personal. Programmatic allegiance is based on considerations of policy, personal allegiance on affection for or loyalty to a particular political leader. In modern nontotalitarian states, both types are usually present to some extent. If we classify societies in terms of the degree to which their members' political allegiances are determined by programmatic or personal considerations, Japan would rank towards the personal end of such a scale. Until rather recently, political programs—reasonably intelligible and meaningful statements of policy—did not have much to do with determining the political attitudes and behavior of the vast majority of Japanese.

With the advent, after the war, of sizable Socialist and Communist parties that provided some measure of real policy choice to the voter, this situation was somewhat altered, and it seems probable that the policy or programmatic content of Japanese politics is still slowly increasing. But, on balance, the mass of the population seems more responsive to personal than to policy appeals and loyalties. Politics in Japan has always been a highly personalized process, in which individual, family, and clan relationships have been of predominant importance. The aspirant to political office normally joined *someone* rather than some cause or policy-oriented movement. In general, this continues to be the case—both within the seemingly more modern and program-oriented left-wing parties as well as in the more traditional conservative ones. As a consequence, the nation's prevailing image of politics is predominantly personal rather than programmatic.

Decision Making

Different peoples also have different views about how political decisions should be made, and these affect the form and operations of their political system. In the United States, for example, we tend to believe that public issues are best decided by an adversary process in which representatives of competing political groups present alternative proposals to the public or their representatives. A majority or plurality of the group then decides the issue, usually by voting, and the defeated minority is expected to acquiesce in the decision or, at least, to engage only in legally recognized forms of protest against it. The traditionally approved form of decision making in Japan is quite different from this. It operates by consensus, which is to say by unanimous consent. Consider what happens when an issue is posed before a group for decision. The problem is discussed at length, but in a nonadversary context. Care is taken to minimize open conflict or debate between the sponsors of alternative solutions. Instead, the group will talk around the issues until at last the nature of a compromise solution acceptable to all parties emerges. This will then be formulated by some senior member as a proposal for action, which will then be accepted by the group by unanimous agreement.

In such a process, there is no open confrontation of groups or parties, no voting in the sense of distinguishing "yeas" from "nays," and, consequently, no open identification of majority and minority elements. The "face" of all participants is guarded, and no one is labeled as being opposed to the solution adopted and, thus, as having broken the harmony of the group or community. Obviously, this is, in theory at least, quite a different system from our own. We assume the existence of majority and minority elements on any serious problem and try to build a constructive role for the minority into our decision-making system. The Japanese system abhors the element of contention involved in the Western system, has no place for open minority elements, and prefers to proceed by compromises that will permit at least the show of unanimity.

This traditional preference for decision by consensus has, of course, long been breaking down in Japan. Particularly in postwar times, the creation of a semi-British type of parliamentary structure and procedure has introduced openly partisan debate, voting, and other adversary techniques into the National Diet. Still, behind the scenes at the national level and far more openly at the local level, it is surprising to see how strong the traditional preference for decision by consensus is. When the opposition forces in Japanese politics complain so bitterly against "tyranny by the majority," they are saying, in effect, that majorities, even when acting by a perfectly legal process, have no right to make a decision which ignores or overrides the views of the minority. The appeal is clearly to the traditional Japanese doctrine of decision by consensus. Not infrequently, aggrieved minorities will resort to violence and rioting in support of such an interpretation.

We should note briefly two other characteristics of the Japanese system of decision making which are related to this matter of consensus. One is the Japanese preference for collective decisions rather than individual ones. The Japanese seem to feel much more comfortable with decisions that are the product of committees or groups than with those of some single leader. The difference is, of course, one of degree, but there is decidedly less emphasis on individual "leaders" and "leadership" as a means of decision making in Japanese culture than in our own. Their political system is even more committee-ridden and group-oriented than is ours. From this system flows the second characteristic: In Japanese politics, blurred compromises often take the place of forceful decisions. This again is true of many modern political systems including our own, but the role of consensus and committees in Japan makes it particularly conspicuous there. Thus clear-cut decisions are difficult to achieve in Japan on any but the most urgent issues.

Political Violence

Peoples vary, too, in their conceptions of the role of violence in domestic politics. In the United States, we usually deny that private violence has any proper place in politics, although developments in the civil rights controversy cast some doubt upon this. Assassination, in particular, seems to most of us a particularly reprehensible political tactic. The Japanese political record is a strange mixture of docility and violence. Japan's history was strongly militarist in its values, of course, for many centuries prior to 1945. Violence and the use of armed force to accomplish political ends have a long and honorable tradition, which is by no means limited to pre-Restoration times. The phrase "government by assassination" gained broad currency in Japan as late as the 1930's, and with considerable justification. Furthermore, it is hard to deny that a very large segment of the populace viewed with tolerance, if not active approbation, the allegedly patriotic assassinations of those days. Such approbation was even more probable if an assassin expiated his crime in the traditionally approved fashion of suicide, preferably by *seppuku* (that is, *hara-kiri*), or if he protested sincere and patriotic motives.

This type of sincerity is of the greatest importance in Japanese politics. If one acts sincerely, that is, through pure and personally disinterested motives, and if one is willing to pay an appropriate price for such action—such as suicide or execution in more serious cases—there is in Japan a traditional inclination to approve both the actor and his act. It is hard to say that this attitude has disappeared in postwar Japan. The violence of numerous so-called "demonstrations" by opposition elements both in the streets and on the floor of the National Diet would seem to indicate that it is still very much alive. "Sincerity" continues to excuse a great deal in Japanese politics.

Tradition versus Change

All societies, including even the most tradition-bound, are constantly changing. Strictly speaking, it is therefore somewhat misleading to pose tradition versus change as if the former implied a rigidly static and unchanging community. But societies differ greatly in their rates of change, the areas and sequences in which change takes place, and, most importantly, in their views of the possibility of change. In Japan, there has certainly been a spate of profound and basic changes during the last century, and especially since her defeat in 1945. Japanese culture as a whole has definitely not been inhospitable to change. Despite this, however, a surprising amount of the traditional survives in Japanese culture, perhaps more in attitudes and behavior than in institutions, and more in the political sector of the society than elsewhere. A mounting struggle has been going on since the end of the war between traditional and modernizing elements in the Japanese political system, and this has profoundly affected national attitudes toward the possibility of political change.

Postwar Japan has seen a rapid acceleration of change. In prewar politics, the balance of power lay normally with conservative and traditionally oriented forces, which were opposed to any significant alterations in the basic institutions or power relationships of the Japanese political system. Postwar Japan has experienced a thorough shaking up of these earlier power relationships, and circumstances far more favorable to political change and innovation have appeared. Although large segments of the population are still apathetic and traditional in their attitudes toward further political and social transformation, a great though slow-moving process of fermentation has been set in motion. More and more Japanese are beginning in fragmentary but important ways to conceive of politics as amenable to some degree of popular influence and control, and in so doing they are slowly beginning to think that political change is a natural or, at least, possible goal of political life. This is quite a change from the political apathy, conservatism, and traditionalism which so successfully opposed political innovations in prewar times. It is also a very important fact about current Japanese politics.

The Japanese people are in the process of changing their minds about so simple but basic a proposition as the possibility and desirability of political change. It is still too early to say what the results will be. The developments may not in the long run be either democratic or progressive from our point of view. But the Japanese no longer regard the existing political situation as a part of the order of things, as fixed and unalterable. A more activist attitude is gaining currency, and more and more of Japan's political leaders are becoming aware of this and adjusting their policies and actions accordingly, thus introducing profound changes in both the style and content of Japanese politics.

Chapter 6

POLITICAL DYNAMICS

Between the foundations of the Japanese political system described in the last chapter and its formal decision-making apparatus lies a gap which is bridged in practice by several types of political actors or agents. In this chapter, we will distinguish three major types of such actors: political parties, political interest groups, and political leaders. In most societies, these serve as links between the population, which has certain historical, ecological, social, and ideological characteristics, and the official machinery of government. They bring the great welter of public interests and desires to the attention of the government, which is then called on to deal with these demands. These agents thus serve to transform interests and issues into political action— a role of the greatest political importance.

Elections

Among the most conspicuous of these political actors are political parties. Parties are primarily instruments for mobilizing votes and choosing among aspirants for public office. Since the activities of parties are closely tied to elections, which decide their success or failure, we will discuss parties and elections in tandem, describing first the electoral system in postwar Japan and then the Japanese political parties.

Japan has had a national election system since February 11, 1889, although in the beginning the suffrage was drastically restricted by tax and residence qualifications to a very small portion of the adult male population. Thereafter, it was gradually liberalized; universal manhood suffrage was finally adopted in 1925, and universal adult suffrage—for women as well as for men—in December, 1945. Prior to the Second World War, however, general elections were not of primary political importance in Japan. They determined membership in only the lower house of the Imperial Diet, or Parliament, and that house played but a subsidiary and carefully controlled role in the making of public policies. Since Japan's defeat and the enactment of a new Constitution in 1947, however, this situation has changed radically. Elections are now a fundamental aspect of the Japanese political system.

There are many levels and varieties of elections in contemporary Japan, but by far the most important and dramatic are the general elections of the entire membership of the House of Representatives, the lower house of the National Diet that has steadily increased in significance in postwar Japan. Control of a majority or plurality of its seats is tantamount to control of the entire national executive and administrative machinery of the state, and, in practice, it is victory in a general election that determines which party will succeed in achieving this cherished goal. As a consequence, general elections are both tense and gala occasions in Japan. Tremendous sums are expended—legally and otherwise—on campaigning, publicity, entertainment, and other means of garnering votes and support. All the media of modern mass communications are called into play, and the public is incessantly entreated and harrassed in noisy attempts to gain its support for this or that candidate and party. When on election day the Japanese voter finally declares his choices, it is a decision of the gravest political consequence, comparable in importance to the results of a British general election or the combination of presidential and congressional elections in this country.

The Electoral System

Among the several levels and types of elections which exist in Japan today, we will here confine our attention to general elections for the House of Representatives. There are at the national level, in addition to these, elections of somewhat different types: (1) those that determine membership in the House of Councillors, that is, the upper house of the National Diet, (2) regular referendums on the holders of Supreme Court justiceships, and (3) special referendums or elections on proposed constitutional amendments, although postwar Japan has not yet had such a case. At the local level, the governors and assemblies of prefectures and the mayors and assemblies of cities, towns, and villages are regularly chosen by public election, and provision is also made for special types of elections or referendums in connection with initiative and recall measures. These other national or local elections are not, however, truly central to the Japanese political process in the same degree as are the general elections of the House of Representatives.

The present general electoral system in Japan is based on the Public Offices Election Law of April, 1950, which consolidated several earlier laws in this field. It guarantees the right to vote to practically all Japanese citizens, male or female, who have reached the age of twenty. Candidates for office must be twenty-five. In the case of the House of Representatives, the Constitution prescribes four-year terms for all members. In fact, no postwar Diet has served this full term;

the Cabinet has always dissolved the lower house at some earlier date and thus brought about general elections at intervals ranging from six and a half months to three years and eight months. For the purposes of such elections, the membership of the lower house was until recently set at 467. With the thirty-first general election in January 1967 it became 486. Candidates are returned from a total of 123 (118 before the thirty-first general election) so-called "medium-sized" election districts, each one of which returns from three to five members, with the exception of the special district of the Amami Islands which is represented by but a single member. Despite the fact that several members are returned from all but one of these districts, each elector casts but a single vote. The system has no multiple-voting or proportional representation aspects. It is technically a multimember constituency, single-vote system. Campaigning is legally restricted to a period of thirty days preceding the election, and almost all facets of campaign practice—including finance, personnel, campaign offices, speeches, advertising, and publicity in general—are rigidly, although somewhat ineffectively, regulated by law.

This type of electoral system gives rise to a number of problems and practices that are unfamiliar to Americans. It produces a wide range of rather exotic problems for the practical politician. If, for example, a major party is conducting a general election campaign in a given election district which returns five members, how many candidates should it run—five, four, three, or some smaller number? If it runs too many in proportion to the party's probable popular support in that district, it takes a serious risk of dividing the party's strength too many ways and thus of losing one or more seats to less powerful parties and candidates who mass their smaller total support behind just one or two candidates. If it runs too few candidates, it is, in effect, wasting those votes which exceed the number required to elect this smaller number of candidates, and this excess may be enough to elect still another candidate. The problem is complicated still further by the fact that most major party contenders really run as candidates of a faction within their party rather than of the party itself. For this reason it is often the case that they compete more keenly and bitterly with other candidates nominally of their own party—but actually from other factions therein—than they do with the ostensible opposition.

Once having determined the optimum number of candidates for a given district, how does the party insure an optimal distribution of its total vote among its several candidates? Any excess votes polled by the party's strongest candidates over the number required to insure their election can only detract—and perhaps disastrously—from the votes available to the party's weaker candidates in that district. This creates some very nice problems in the proper apportionment of the vote. The system thus contains a sort of built-in bias in favor of weaker parties and candidates. It forces the majority party to calculate its chances optimistically and constantly tempts it to run too many candidates, thus splitting its strength, while at the same time the system encourages weaker parties to concentrate their smaller support more effectively behind one or two candidates. These are problems not encountered in our own type of single-member constituencies.

Many Japanese, especially in the Liberal-Democratic Party, feel that this electoral system maximizes factionalism and disunity within a political party, adversely affects the quality of leadership that parties can provide for the country, places a premium on local as opposed to national electoral issues and on considerations of personality rather than of policy, and is conducive to an unnecessary and highly undesirable amount of electoral corruption and campaign abuses. As a consequence there is a good deal of current discussion of possible changes and improvements through the adoption of a small-district, single-member, single-vote system or some modified version of this incorporating features of proportional representation. Politically, however, few institutions are more difficult to change than electoral systems and it has not so far been possible to obtain the needed degree of consensus, even within the ranks of the majority party.

Along more familiar lines, the Japanese electoral system, like our own, has failed to keep abreast of large-scale shifts in residence within Japan. Until July, 1964, there had been no reapportionment of seats to compensate for the much more rapid growth of population in the cities than in the countryside. The population of the city of Tokyo, for example, more than doubled in the ten years between 1950 and 1960, whereas that of many of the more rural prefectures and election districts actually declined. Yet there had been no increase at all in the number of members representing Tokyo in the House of Representatives. As a consequence, the actual political value of a Japanese elector's vote varied enormously depending on where he lived. It was worth, for example, approximately three times as much if he was a resident of Hyogo Prefecture's rural and stable Fifth Election District than if he lived in Tokyo's First District. The more glaring examples of such malapportionment were somewhat improved by a very partial reapportionment law enacted in July, 1964, that added five new electoral districts and nineteen new seats to five of the most underrepresented metropolitan areas. But many inequities and discrepancies remain.

Electoral Participation

Among nations where voting is not compulsory, Japan has a very high rate of electoral participation. The great majority of those who are eligible do ordinarily vote. The latest available compilation of the national list of qualified electors, that of January 1967, shows that a total of 62,992,906 Japanese were then entitled to vote (Table 6-1). This represented 61 per cent of the total population of Japan. In the 1967 general election 45,996,561 of those then eligible to do so (or 73.99 per cent of the qualified voters) cast valid ballots. This was the third lowest turnout for such an election since 1947. It still compares very favorably with the 60–64 per cent of our own adult population who have voted in recent presidential elections.

By American standards, it is also interesting to note in Table 6-1 that rural voting turnouts in Japan are uniformly and appreciably higher than urban, and that electoral participation increases as one goes down the scale from national through prefectural to local elections. In both cities and countryside, a local assembly election has usually brought out anywhere from 85 to 95 per cent of the eligible voters. Both of these phenomena reverse the usual American experience. The higher voting rate in the countryside is primarily explained by the greater political docility and mobilizability of farm as opposed to city voters, plus the fact that failure to vote, which is socially disapproved, is hard to conceal from one's friends and neighbors in the countryside, whereas urban

TABLE 6-1

PERCENTAGE OF QUALIFIED VOTERS PARTICIPATING IN POSTWAR ELECTIONS

Election	HOUSE OF REPRESENTATIVES Percentage voting			Number of qualified voters	HOUSE OF COUNCILLORS Percentage voting		PREFECTURAL ASSEMBLIES Percentage voting			LOCAL ASSEMBLIES Percentage voting		
	Total	Urban	Rural		National constituency	Local constituencies	Total	Urban	Rural	Assemblies of the five great cities	City assemblies	Town and village assemblies
1947	67.95			40,907,493	60.93	61.12	81.65			a	a	81.17
1949	74.04			42,105,300								
1950				43,461,371	72.19	72.19						
1951				44,230,610			82.99			72.92	90.56	95.92
1952	76.43			46,772,584								
1953	74.22	66.06	80.23	47,090,167	63.18	63.18						
1955	75.84	71.90	80.60	49,235,375			77.24			62.26	85.00	92.33
1956				50,177,888	62.10	62.11						
1958	76.99	74.19	81.18	52,013,529								
1959				53,516,473	58.74	58.75	79.48	76.41	84.75	65.09	85.81	92.50
1960	73.51			54,312,993								
1962				56,137,295	68.21	68.22						
1963	71.14			58,281,678			76.85	73.63	83.72	65.60	82.32	91.50
1965				59,542,585	67.01	67.01						
1967	73.99			62,992,906								

a These figures are included in the town and village figure for 1947.

56

residence provides a measure of anonymity in this respect. The greater appeal of local elections also seems to be due to the survival of traditional views of one's village, town, fief, or other local unit as the arena of most meaningful political interests and loyalties. These older identifications have not yet been effectively superseded by a more modern focus on the nation as the prime claimant of popular political interest and allegiance. Such a transfer is gradually in process, however.

The Electoral Record

Against this background, let us examine the results of the nine general elections held in Japan since the enactment of the new Constitution in 1947 (see Table 6-2). There have, of course, been a number of political parties involved during this period and, as the result of splits and amalgamations, some of these no longer exist as independent units. For introductory purposes, therefore, it may be more satisfactory to talk first in terms of "conservative" versus "progressive," or left-wing, parties and consider these as units, and then to define the parties more precisely.

The most notable fact about the Japanese electoral record is the continuous and strong predominance of the conservative vote. This was even more true before the war. Since 1947, the conservative share of the popular vote—which includes the bulk of the independent votes as well as those cast specifically for conservatives—has not fallen below fifty-four per cent of the total nor has the number of seats in the lower house controlled by conservatives fallen below fifty-eight per cent. The combined "progressive," or left-wing, opposition parties share most of the remaining votes, which range from about twenty-five to forty per cent, and the remaining seats in the House of Representatives, which range from nineteen to thirty-seven per cent. The difference in the strengths of the two groups is thus very large. In recent years, the conservatives have normally controlled about three-fifths of the popular vote and seats, while the progressives as a group have been approaching two-fifths. Although the curve of progressive strength has on the whole gone up slightly since 1947 and that of conservative (including independent) strength has declined a bit, the change has been too slight to have a significant effect on the distribution of political power. In this fact lies the present dilemma of Japanese socialism.

This conservative predominance in the lower house of the National Diet is somewhat less marked in the upper house. The electoral system for the House of Councillors is more complicated than that of the House of Representatives, and a direct comparison of popular voting patterns for the two houses would take some time. In terms of percentages of seats won in recent elections for the upper house, however, the progressives have done no better than they have in the lower house. The conservatives have normally controlled about three-fifths of the total number of seats here, too. In the elections for prefectural governors and assemblies and for city, town, and village mayors or assemblies, the conservative cause is even stronger. At these levels, independent candidates and voters are almost uniformly conservative. It is not surprising, then, that the records of recent elections show that at the prefectural assembly level in the postwar years the progressive parties have never polled more than twenty-nine per cent of the national vote nor controlled more than twenty-three per cent of the seats. Their average strength has been appreciably lower than this.

It is at the lowest level—city, town, and village assemblies—however, that the greatest display of conservative strength is found. Here the best showing by progressive candidates in city assembly elections amounted to seventeen per cent of the votes cast nationally and thirteen per cent of the seats at stake. In elections for town and village assemblies the combined progressive showing was even poorer—four per cent of the total vote and three per cent of the seats. At these local levels also, the curve of progressive strength has been slowly mounting in recent elections, but conservative strength continues to be overwhelming. As one descends the scale of elections in Japan, therefore, from national through prefectural to municipal or local elections, conservative strength, dominant to begin with, is seen to increase markedly at each step downward, while progressive strength—socialist plus Communist—diminishes *pari passu*. The electoral record will also demonstrate that conservative strength, although dominant even in the cities, is most strongly entrenched in the rural areas of Japan. The cities, and particularly the ranks of organized labor, provide the strongest electoral support for progressive candidates and causes, whereas the real heartland of conservative political strength lies in the countryside.

Where particular party strengths are concerned, Table 6-2 will make clear the nature of the electoral record in postwar times. Since 1955, the conservative cause has been represented by a single party—really a loose congeries of factions—called the *Jiyuminshuto* or Liberal Democratic Party. This group dominates the electoral scene today, as, in a variety of earlier forms, it has done almost continuously since 1945. The dimensions of its strength have been described above. The progressive vote is somewhat more complicated to analyze. Socialist and Communist components have always been identifiable within the progressive bloc, and frequently several other types of organizations as well.

Since January, 1960—after some five years of dubious unity—it has become necessary to separate the electoral record of the *Shakaito,* or Socialist Party proper, from that of the *Minshu Shakaito,* or Democratic (right-wing) Socialist Party. The former emerged from the 1960 elections as much the stronger of the two Socialist groups, winning twenty-eight per cent of the vote and thirty-one per cent of the seats, as opposed to the latter's nine per cent of the votes and four per cent of the seats. The Democratic Socialist Party did not notably improve upon this performance in the 1963 general election but made a promising comeback in the 1967 election.

The Communist Party has never had much electoral strength in Japan. It has normally polled only between two and five per cent of the votes in general elections and held no more than one per cent of the seats in the House of Representatives. The one occasion, in 1949, when it significantly improved on this performance occurred under most unusual circumstances and is not to be considered as an accurate representation of the party's actual strength. This low level of popular support for Communist candidates has not changed appreciably since the 1949 election.

More recently, another political party has emerged in Japan. It is known as the *Komeito,* or Fair Play Party, and first began to run candidates for national office in a formal sense in the 1956 House of Councillors Elections. In 1962 it succeeded in electing nine of its candidates and another eleven were returned in the 1965 upper house elections. It is now, therefore, the third largest party in the House of Councillors. Until 1967 the *Komeito* refrained from participation in elections for the lower house of the National Diet but in that year it ran thirty-two candidates and succeeded in acquiring twenty-five seats. The Fair Play Party is unique among present-day Japanese parties in that it is the political arm of a nominally Buddhist religious sect, the *Sokagak-kai,* a so-called "new religion" that has gained great strength in the past decade or so and currently claims a following of some fifteen million communicants.

Political independents and minor parties, other than the foregoing groups, do not at present play a significant role in Japanese elections at the national level. There have been several minor parties, such as the *Kokumin Kyodoto* (People's Cooperative Party) in the conservative camp and the *Ronoto* (Labor-Farmer Party) on the progressive side, which have since the war managed to survive for appreciable periods of time, but the dynamics of the recent political process have run against them. Unlike the Communists, they have lacked both a readily distinguishable program with stable appeal to at least a significant minority and an effective party organization. It remains to be seen, incidentally, whether the Democratic Socialists and the Fair Play Party can come up with effective and durable programs and organizations. The other minor parties have tended to represent the personal followings of individual politicians organized into cliques of more than usual independence and durability rather than parties in the present Japanese sense of the term. They have disappeared through absorption into the major conservative and progressive parties, a normal fate for recent minor parties in Japan.

The role of the independent candidate in national elections is also no longer very significant. Almost all such candidates are conservatives, who, because of real or fancied tactical advantages in their particular districts, choose to campaign as political independents. Once elected—and few are—their normal practice is to make at once the best possible deal with the Liberal Democratic Party leadership and formally become members of this parliamentary group, thus exchanging their independent status for that of "loyal" conservative party followers. At the level of prefectural and, particularly, local elections, that is, for mayors and assemblymen in cities, towns, and villages, where national party labels are far less useful and meaningful, there continues to be a great number of "independent" candidates, the vast majority of whom are conservatives in fact. The 1963 local elections, for example, awarded about thirteen per cent of the seats in prefectural assemblies and ninety-five per cent of those in town and village assemblies to such so-called "independent" candidates.

Japan's postwar electoral record is marked, therefore, by a heavy and continuous dominance of conservative candidates and causes at all levels of government. It should not be assumed, however, that this is an immutable characteristic of Japanese society. Such circumstances as the American Occupation, which continued officially until 1952, Japan's peculiar relationship to the Korean conflict, from 1950 to 1953, and the increasing prosperity of the revived Japanese economy after 1952 have spurred this conservative political ascendancy. During this period, Japan has been unusually sheltered from the full stress of the cold war and its attendant international tensions. She has yet to experience, in post-Occupation times, a serious or prolonged economic depression.

TABLE 6-2
RESULTS OF POSTWAR GENERAL ELECTIONS FOR JAPAN'S HOUSE OF REPRESENTATIVES

Party	23RD GENERAL ELECTION (1947)				24TH GENERAL ELECTION (1949)				25TH GENERAL ELECTION (1952)				26TH GENERAL ELECTION (1953)			
	Valid votes	Percentage of votes	Seats	Percentage of seats	Valid votes	Percentage	Seats	Percentage	Valid votes	Percentage	Seats	Percentage	Valid votes	Percentage	Seats	Percentage
Conservatives (subtotal)	16,111,914	58.9	281	60.3	19,260,500	63.0	347	74.5	23,367,671	66.1	325	69.6	22,717,348	65.7	310	66.5
Jiyuto (Liberal Party)	7,356,321	26.9	131	28.1					16,938,221	47.9	240	51.4				
Minshuto (Democratic Party)	6,839,646	25.0	121	26.0	4,798,352	15.7	69	14.8								
Kokumin Kyodoto (People's Cooperative Party)	1,915,947	7.0	29	6.2	1,041,879	3.4	14	3.0								
Minshu Jiyuto (Democratic Liberal Party)					13,420,269	43.9	264	56.7								
Kaishinto (Progressive Party)									6,429,450	18.2	85	18.2	6,186,232	17.9	76	16.3
Hatoyama Jiyuto (Hatoyama Liberal Party)													3,054,688	8.8	35	7.5
Yoshida Jiyuto (Yoshida Liberal Party)													13,476,428	39.0	199	42.7
Jiyu Minshuto (Liberal Democratic Party)																
Progressives (subtotal)	8,178,842	29.9	147	31.5	7,721,414	25.2	90	19.3	8,664,826	24.5	115	24.7	10,209,311	29.5	144	30.9
Shakaito (Socialist Party)	7,175,939	26.2	143	30.7	4,129,794	13.5	48	10.3								
Saha Shakaito (Left-wing Socialist Party)									3,398,597	9.6	54	11.6	4,516,715	13.1	72	15.4
Uha Shakaito (Right-wing Socialist Party)									4,108,274	11.6	57	12.2	4,677,833	13.5	66	14.2
Ronoto (Labor-Farmer Party)					606,840	2.0	7	1.5	261,190	0.7	4	0.9	358,773	1.0	5	1.1
Minshu Shakaito (Democratic Socialist Party)																
Kyosanto (Communist Party)	1,002,903	3.7	4	0.8	2,984,780	9.7	35	7.5	896,765	2.6	—	—	655,990	1.9	1	0.2
Minor Parties	1,490,057	5.4	25	5.4	1,602,496	5.2	17	3.6	949,036	2.7	7	1.5	152,050	0.4	1	0.2
Independents	1,580,844	5.8	13	2.8	2,008,109	6.6	12	2.6	2,355,172	6.7	19	4.1	1,523,736	4.4	11	2.4
Totals	27,361,657	100.0	466	100.0	30,592,519	100.0	466	100.0	35,336,705	100.0	466	100.0	34,602,445	100.0	466	100.0

TABLE 6-2

RESULTS OF POSTWAR GENERAL ELECTIONS FOR JAPAN'S HOUSE OF REPRESENTATIVES—(Continued)

Party	27TH GENERAL ELECTION (1955)				28TH GENERAL ELECTION (1958)				29TH GENERAL ELECTION (1960)				30TH GENERAL ELECTION (1963)				31ST GENERAL ELECTION (1967)			
	Valid votes	Percentage of votes	Seats	Percentage of seats	Valid votes	Percentage	Seats	Percentage	Valid votes	Percentage	Seats	Percentage	Valid votes	Percentage	Seats	Percentage	Valid votes	Percentage	Seats	Percentage
Conservatives (subtotal)	23,385,502	63.2	297	63.6	22,976,846	57.8	287	61.5	22,740,272	57.5	296	63.3	22,423,915	54.7	283	60.6	22,447,834	48.8	277	57.0
Jiyuto (Liberal Party)	9,849,457	26.6	112	24.0																
Minshuto (Democratic Party)	13,536,044	36.6	185	39.6																
Kokumin Kyodoto (People's Cooperative Party)																				
Minshu Jiyuto (Democratic Liberal Party)																				
Kaishinto (Progressive Party)																				
Hatoyama Jiyuto (Hatoyama Liberal Party)																				
Yoshida Jiyuto (Yoshida Liberal Party)																				
Jiyu Minshuto (Liberal Democratic Party)					22,976,846	57.8	287	61.5	22,740,272	57.5	296	63.3	22,423,915	54.7	283	60.6	22,447,834	48.8	277	57.0
Progressives (subtotal)	11,903,639	32.2	162	34.7	14,106,028	35.5	167	35.7	15,508,005	39.2	165	35.2	16,576,545	40.4	172	36.7	18,421,124	40.1	175	36.0
Shakaito (Socialist Party)					13,093,993	32.9	166	35.5	10,887,134	27.5	145	31.0	11,906,766	29.0	144	30.8	12,826,099	27.9	140	28.8
Saha Shakaito (Left-wing Socialist Party)	5,683,312	15.3	89	19.1																
Uha Shakaito (Right-wing Socialist Party)	5,129,594	13.9	67	14.3																
Ronoto (Labor-Farmer Party)	357,611	1.0	4	0.9																
Minshu Shakaito (Democratic Socialist Party)					1,012,035	2.6	1	0.6	3,464,148	8.7	17	3.6	3,023,302	7.4	23	4.9	3,404,462	7.4	30	6.2
Kyosanto (Communist Party)	733,121	2.0	2	0.4	287,991	0.7	1	0.2	1,156,723	2.9	3	0.6	1,646,477	4.0	5	1.0	2,190,563	4.8	5	1.0
Komeito (Fair Play Party)																	2,472,371	5.4	25	5.1
Minor Parties	496,614	1.3	2	0.4					141,941	0.3	1	0.2	59,765	0.1	0	0.0	101,244	0.2	0	0.0
Independents	1,229,081	3.3	6	1.3	2,380,795	6.0	12	2.6	1,118,905	2.8	5	1.0	1,956,313	4.8	12	2.5	2,553,988	5.5	9	1.9
Totals	37,014,837	100.0	467	100.0	39,751,661	100.0	467	100.0	39,509,123	100.0	467	100.0	41,016,540	100.0	467	100.0	45,996,561	100.0	486	100.0

Still, under what have been for them seriously disadvantageous circumstances, the "progressive," or left-wing, parties have managed collectively to acquire more than one-third of the popular vote and of the seats in the powerful lower house of the Diet. This gives them, incidentally, the important power to prevent any adverse amendments of the Japanese Constitution, since such proposals require the concurring vote of two-thirds or more of all the members of each house of the National Diet. This degree of success by the Socialist Party in particular is not to be depreciated. It is impossible to predict the effects on the Japanese electorate of a prolonged depression or a really serious international crisis involving Japanese interests, but the possibility that this would work in favor of the "progressive" cause cannot be discounted.

Political Parties

Political parties are not a postwar innovation in Japan. In one form or another, they have existed since at least 1874. The antecedents of the present conservative party, the *Jiyuminshuto,* or Liberal Democratic Party, can be traced back to the early 1880's, and those of the *Nihon Shakaito,* or Japan Socialist Party, go back to at least 1925. The Japan Communist Party (*Nihon Kyosanto*) was established in 1922. It is, therefore, primarily the status and power of Japan's political parties which have altered in postwar times. From groups competing for the control of membership in a House of Representatives possessed in prewar times of largely negative and carefully restricted political power, they have advanced since 1947 to the status of groups competing for the control of membership in a House of Representatives which has itself become the basic source of both legislative and executive authority in a new and more democratic system of national government. The difference is of vital importance. The role and importance of Japan's political parties have fluctuated with the role and importance of the lower house of the National Diet. The postwar development of these political parties is described in Fig. 6-1.

In this discussion of the organization, programs, and general characteristics of Japan's political parties, we will limit ourselves to the five parties that are most important at present—the Liberal Democratic, Socialist, Democratic Socialist, Communist, and Fair Play parties. Although we cannot be sure how long a given constellation of parties will survive the constant pressures for fission and reconstitution, these five parties represent the major types of organization, programmatic appeals, support patterns, financing, and leadership which have characterized Japan's postwar political parties.

The Liberal Democratic Party (Jiyuminshuto)

It should be made clear at the outset that the Liberal Democratic Party, despite its great strength at the polls, is not essentially a mass membership organization. Although possessed of a national party apparatus which looks most impressive on an organization chart, its formal membership is relatively small. In August, 1966, for example, it claimed a total registered membership of

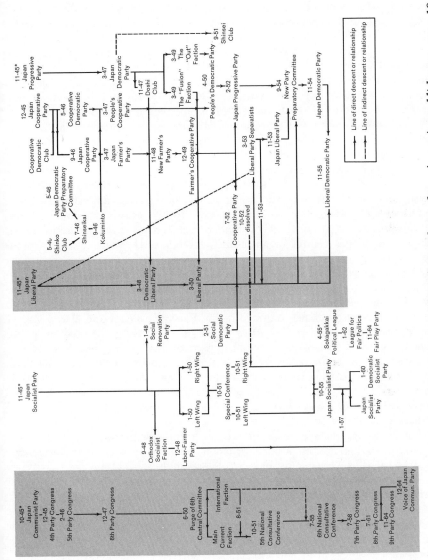
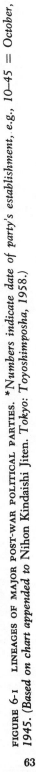

FIGURE 6-1 LINEAGES OF MAJOR POST-WAR POLITICAL PARTIES. *Numbers indicate date of party's establishment, e.g., 10–45 = October, 1945. (Based on chart appended to Nihon Kindaishi Jiten. Tokyo: Toyoshimposha, 1958.)

about 1,700,000. Most commentators believe that a figure in the neighborhood of 350,000 would be more accurate. Indeed, one finds at the local level that formal party membership is a vague and not too meaningful category. The party maintains branch organizations in every prefectural capital and in an increasing number of other cities, towns, and villages. In 1963, in fact, its National Organization Committee claimed to have a total of 2,600 local branches covering about 76 per cent of the 3,422 political subdivisions of Japan plus some 22,000 "party organizers" scattered throughout Japan. This claim may be true if interpreted so as to include those working for its candidates during election campaigns, but it probably has little meaning beyond this. The party is trying to strengthen its prefectural and local organizations throughout the country and thus to establish more meaningful and dependable relationships with the average voter, and it seems to have made some progress along these lines. But, in general, most of its local branches and the great bulk of its membership are concerned primarily with elections and become active or involved as a group only during campaigns.

The heart and head of the Liberal Democratic organization are found in Tokyo, where the vast majority of the party's business is transacted. In fact, for purposes of most policy decisions and day-to-day business, the party is almost exclusively controlled by its higher membership normally resident in Tokyo. The party's central organization is complex. Ultimate authority in a formal sense is wielded by a party congress composed exclusively of professional political leaders. The congress meets annually in Tokyo and every second year selects a party president, the most eminent and powerful of party posts. Of great importance also are the secretary-general, who directs day-to-day party activities, and the chairmen of the Executive Board and of the Policy Board. The thirty-member Executive Board is also very influential in party councils. Through this organizational apparatus and its adjunct committees, the party determines its policies and attempts to translate them into legislative actions through its delegations in the National Diet. Once agreement has been reached within party circles, the discipline imposed on its members in the Diet is very strict. Voting conformance is practically automatic, under pain of expulsion from the party.

The almost complete absence of reliable information about party finances in Japan does not inhibit public discussion of them, usually in rather sensational terms. The general assumption about the Liberal Democratic Party is that a very substantial measure of control over its policies is wielded by its financial supporters, and that these are to be found almost exclusively in the ranks of big business, particularly among the *zaibatsu*, or great cartels of Japan. Few persons familiar with Japanese politics would deny that the party's connections with big business are very close, or that the bulk of its support comes from business firms and associations. But the details of this relationship and the extent of the influence or control over party policies by business interests are very vague and imprecise. The average commentary on the subject tends to overestimate the unity of the political views and programs of "big business" and, consequently, to oversimplify the Liberal Democratic Party's relationship to business.

Party politics—particularly election campaigns—is still a very expensive operation in Japan as elsewhere. We can get a vague and understated idea of the size of the funds involved from the official reports of political contributions which the parties are required by law to file with the Local Autonomy Ministry. These indicate that in 1963, an election year, the Liberal Democratic Party itself received political contributions amounting to 5,383,210,325 yen ($14,953,000), whereas during the politically less active year of 1964 it declared a total income of 2,253,651,141 yen ($6,260,000). But this does not include other categories of revenue that are equally available to the Liberal Democratic Party to meet its electoral and other expenses. For example in 1963, the latest year for which reasonably complete public records are available, the party's several factions admitted to having raised collectively a further 1,911,508,895 yen ($5,309,000). The declared revenue available to the Liberal Democratic Party in 1963 thus totalled 7,294,719,220 yen, or approximately $20,262,000. The bulk of this came in large contributions from the Citizens' Association (*Kokumin Kyokai*), a separately incorporated fund-raising arm of the Party, or from business firms or associations. Even by American standards these are not unimpressive amounts, particularly when we realize that they constitute but an unknown fraction of the total political funds available to the party during that year. In addition to these open and publicized contributions, it is widely believed that a large amount was probably raised covertly by the party, by factions within the party, and by individual candidates who had access to their own private sources of campaign funds. The actual total, then, although not ascertainable, is certainly formidable. One recent commentator, for example, estimates the total expenditure of the Liberal Democrats in the earlier and cheaper 1960 general election campaign at about 4,000,-000,000 yen ($11,111,111) or an average of 10,000,000 yen ($27,778) per candidate. Clearly, it costs a great deal of money to conduct effectively the affairs of a major political party in Japan.

It is particularly difficult to describe accurately the leadership of the Liberal Democratic Party. Superficially, the party is led by its president who, since this is normally the majority party, is also the Prime Minister of Japan. But when we look more closely, we soon see that the Liberal Democratic Party really has no single leader. In fact, it is in some ways more accurate to view it as a loose coalition of factions united for purposes of campaign and legislative strategy, rather than as a unified national party. In 1966, for example, when Sato Eisaku was party president and Prime Minister, the party was actually divided into some thirteen major factions. These groups were composed of members of the party holding seats in the National Diet, and in the lower house they ranged in size from about four to fifty-one individuals. Practically all the party's delegation in the House belonged to one or the other of them. These factions were led by prominent politicians who regarded themselves as quite the equal of Mr. Sato and most of them aspired to both the party presidency and the premiership. All factions were based on considerations of personal loyalty and advantage rather than principle or policy.

The balance of power within the party—and, consequently, the immediate explanation of most party appointments and to a lesser degree, policies—is determined primarily by shifting combinations and agreements among the leaders of these factions. It normally takes a common front among at least four of them to carry any important decision. As a result, their leaders are very important figures. Four or five of them in combination can normally make or break a Cabinet. From this we can conclude, first, that a successful party president and Prime Minister must accommodate himself to their advice and wishes; second, that party leadership is really more a collegial than an individual matter; and, third, that most major decisions taken by the party on issues of policy or appointment represent rather complicated compromises. On most important questions, a sizable and organized element within the Liberal Democratic Party is certain to be actively dissatisfied with prevailing party policy. Such opposition, although it may occasionally abstain or absent itself from the House, will seldom be carried so far as to produce a vote against the party line. This might lead to the disintegration of the party which, at present only a few seem really to desire. But the existence of a constant and organized minority does serve to keep the party in a volatile and uncertain state. Decisive or durable individual leadership over a period of time is very difficult under these circumstances.

The leadership of the Liberal Democratic Party—as represented by its members holding seats in the lower house of the National Diet—may also be analyzed in terms of the members' social and professional backgrounds. A 1963 survey of the lower house yields the following information, which is fairly typical for recent years. With allowances for multiple and overlapping backgrounds, about twenty-five per cent of the party's lower house delegation of 300 individuals were former career bureaucrats who had held high office in the national or prefectural governments. An appreciable but unstated number had also once served as prefectural assemblymen, or had held elective offices at the city, town, or village level. Whatever their previous experience, the Liberal Democratic members of the lower house in 1963 had been elected to this office an average of five times. They were experienced professional politicians. A large number, forty per cent, had business backgrounds, usually as presidents, auditors, or directors of firms. About nine per cent had been connected with various professional associations, another nine per cent were journalists, and eight per cent were lawyers. Considering the agrarian basis of the party's support, surprisingly few representatives professed agricultural backgrounds, less than two per cent in fact.

None had a labor-union background. Nearly four-fifths were college graduates, thirty-five per cent from Tokyo University. For the entire group, 1905 was the average year of birth, making their average age fifty-eight in 1963.

These figures point up several matters that are widely discussed in Japan today. Besides the alleged domination of the party by business interests, many claim that ex-bureaucrats, especially those from Tokyo University, wield an undue and dangerous influence in the higher councils of the Liberal Democratic Party. It is undoubtedly true that former bureaucrats, because of their professional skills and associations, have been notably successful within the party. In fact, all conservative Prime Ministers in postwar times, except Mr. Hatoyama and Mr. Ishibashi, have been former career bureaucrats. Critics of this phenomenon charge that the experience of these individuals in the prewar bureaucracy has made them authoritarian in training and temperament, reactionary in political persuasion, and generally undemocratic in their methods and policies. Although there is undoubtedly some truth in such claims, we should not forget that the largely socialist critics differ fundamentally with the conservatives over the nature of a democratic society.

The program of the Liberal Democratic Party, of course, changes with the issues that are current at any given time. It also represents the product of numerous compromises and is in many respects as cautiously vague in its stands and promises as are the programs of our own major parties. It is not, by American standards, a notably conservative document. During the upper house election of July, 1965, for example, it called for the signing of a treaty establishing normal diplomatic relations with South Korea; a fair, negotiated settlement of the hostilities in Vietnam; the promotion of economic and cultural—but not political—relations with the Chinese People's Republic; support for the security treaty with the United States; the improvement of social welfare programs, including the realization of the "one family, one home" program by 1970; an expanded program of road and highway construction and repair; controlled economic growth with stabilization of prices paid by consumers; governmental support for the modernization of agriculture, fisheries, and small and medium industries; and a large-scale tax reduction.

Of these, by far the most controversial stands were those favoring the Korean treaty and continued close association with the United States. In general, the program was solicitous of public welfare, pointed with pride to the general prosperity which the party's regime had brought to Japan, and promised to produce more of the same.

The Japan Socialist Party (Nihon Shakaito)

Although socialist and left-wing political parties existed in Japan before the war, they were of small electoral or parliamentary significance. Only since 1945 have they constituted the major opposition to the dominant conservative groups. For one brief nine-month period in 1947–48, they were even able to obtain the leadership of a weak coalition Cabinet for their current leader, Katayama Tetsu. The Japan Socialist Party in its present form dates from October, 1955, when its formerly separate left- and right-wing factions were merged into a single party. The party remains more or less unified, although a portion of the right-wing contingent seceded in January, 1960, to form the Democratic Socialist Party. Like the conservatives, the Socialists are not a mass party. A recent report indicates a total party membership of slightly over fifty thousand, organized in more than 1,300 local branches, special districts, and factory branches throughout Japan; local organizations exist, therefore, in somewhat more than one-third of Japan's 3,422 prefectures, cities, towns, and villages. These membership claims are probably somewhat inflated, if we apply a regular dues-paying test. The inadequate contacts of the party with the voting populace, particularly in the villages and countryside, are a source of serious concern to the party, and it is taking modest steps to improve this situation. So far, these have not paid any very spectacular dividends, but slow progress is doubtless being made.

Like the apparatus of their Liberal Democratic rivals, that of the Japan Socialist Party is highly centralized in Tokyo, where an elaborate party headquarters is maintained. The party has no president but is headed by the chairman of its central executive committee. Its administrative chief is the secretary-general, and the chairman of its control committee also plays an important role in the party. Ultimate authority within the party resides theoretically in an annual party congress, which is usually a far more lively and controversial affair than its Liberal Democratic counterpart. The congress elects the party's chief officers and it debates vociferously such long-standing policy issues as whether the party should represent national interests or class interests, that is, those of the industrial and peasant proletariats; what attitude it should adopt toward Communists and the Japan Communist Party; and what relationship the party should maintain with the unions and federations of unions which provide the bulk of its support. In addition to the party congress, the conference of party members who hold seats in the National Diet also plays an important role in the party councils. As with the conservatives, this body—once a party policy has been established—is under rigid obligation to provide loyal and unanimous voting support for the party's legislative program in both houses.

The Japan Socialist Party obviously does not command the financial resources or support that the Liberal Democratic Party does. The available figures are incomplete but they indicate, for example, that during the election year of 1963 the Socialist Party received a total of 428,727,191 yen ($1,190,000). This does not compare very favorably with the 7,294,719,220 yen ($20,262,-000) in campaign funds reported by the Liberal Democrats during the same period. A report on campaign expenditures during the earlier 1960 general election estimated that the Socialist Party probably spent in the neighborhood of 460,000,000 yen ($1,277,777) or about 2,500,000 yen ($6,944) per candidate. The total is only 11 per cent of the estimated expenditures of the Liberal Democrats in the same campaign.

The pattern of contributions to the Socialists' campaign funds is also different from that of the Liberal Democrats. The largest single contributor by far is *Sohyo*, the General Council of Japanese Labor Unions. About half of the reported funds in the 1960 election came in contributions of more than 3,000,000 yen ($8,333), and the remainder were mostly much smaller contributions. An undetermined but major portion of the party's financial support comes from labor unions, but a number of big businesses also contribute—though much less heavily—to the Socialists as well as to the Liberal Democrats. Thus the businessmen hope to maintain credit in both camps. Ideally, the Socialist Party hopes to improve its shaky financial position by recruiting as many as two hundred thousand members willing to pay annual dues of 200 to 300 yen (56 to 83 cents), but to date they have not had any striking success in collecting a small annual dues from even their present membership of 52,200.

Within the Japan Socialist Party, several factions are constantly vying for control. At present, at least five or six such factions are readily identifiable. Although these factions resemble somewhat those in the Liberal Democratic Party, ideology is far more important in distinguishing one faction from another in the Socialist Party than in the Liberal Democratic Party. In fact, the Socialist groups range from the Right through the Center to the Left of the Socialist spectrum. The party's factions thus continue to reflect the pre-1955 situation when the Socialists were actually split into separate left- and right-wing parties. The party leadership is still highly unstable, and the clashing ideological stands of the several factions indicate a very serious lack of unity on both doctrinal and tactical matters within the party. As with the Liberal

Democrats, policy in the Socialist Party is a product of continual pulling and hauling among the leaders of the conflicting factions.

An examination of the backgrounds of the Socialist leaders reveals that they have quite different careers from those of their Liberal Democratic rivals. Among the 168 Socialist members of the lower house in the 1958–60 period, only four per cent were former career bureaucrats. A sizable group—twenty-nine per cent—had served as prefectural assemblymen or elected officials in cities, towns, and villages. Many members had had prior experience in national legislative service, having been elected to the lower house an average of 3.8 times. Eighteen per cent of the 168 had some form of business background, and ten per cent had served as leaders of agricultural cooperative associations or had some other type of agricultural affiliation. By far the largest number, however—some fifty per cent—had risen from union backgrounds, most from labor unions but a fair number from farmers' unions as well. Sixty-two per cent were college graduates, divided almost equally between national and private universities. Their average year of birth was 1906; thus their average age was fifty-two at the beginning of this Diet. In the new Diet established in 1963 this average age had risen to fifty-four.

This profile of the average Socialist representative points up some of the principal differences between the Socialists and the Liberal Democrats. Whereas the former come primarily from union backgrounds, the latter come from the ranks of business. Again, former bureaucrats are very prominent and influential among the conservative group but almost entirely lacking in the Socialist ranks. The members of the Socialist leadership group are also generally several years younger than their Liberal Democratic counterparts. On the other hand, both groups tend to be college educated, to underrepresent the agrarian sector of the population, and to contain a substantial element of former local assemblymen and officials. Members of both groups have also become highly professionalized and experienced as party politicians. In most cases, party office is a career for them, not an avocation.

Although the Socialist Party has gone to some pains to develop a rounded program covering both domestic and foreign matters, its foreign policy has attracted the greatest attention and proved to be both its greatest asset and its most controversial plank. For many years, the Socialist Party has opposed the fundamentally pro-United States and pro-Western orientation of Japan's official foreign policy. There are serious differences of opinion within the party, however, as to how this stand should be implemented. Some view the United States as an aggressive, imperialist power and the prime enemy of socialist causes throughout the world. Others are more moderate and would prefer to maintain friendly political, economic, and cultural relations with the United States, the Chinese People's Republic, and the U.S.S.R. There is a continuous struggle about how either policy should be activated and at what pace, but in recent years the Socialist Party has officially advocated the abrogation of the United States–Japanese Security Treaty, the complete withdrawal of American armed forces, and some rather vague measure of demilitarization and disarmament for Japan. The party also favors the admission of mainland China to the United Nations, Japanese recognition of the Peking government, and the conclusion of formal treaties of peace with China and the Soviet Union (neither of which are signatories of the Treaty of San Francisco which in 1951 concluded the war with Japan). During 1964–65 the Socialists also campaigned vigorously against the conclusion of a treaty with the Republic of Korea.

Since all these steps run counter to the policies to which the Liberal Democratic government of Japan is officially committed at present, there have been frequent and dramatic encounters between the Socialists and the government on all of these scores. Mass demonstrations, riots, and violence have erupted in both the streets and the parliament, and have spurred a great deal of popular interest and debate both in Japan and throughout the world.

The domestic policies of the Socialist Party have attracted less attention. In 1965, for example, the party advocated some rather vague measure of nationalization of basic industries, stabilization of the prices of both food and land, improvements in the social insurance and old-age pension plans, elimination of the discrepancies between incomes and standards of living in rural and urban areas, an increase in the number of higher schools, support for local autonomy in the face of persistent encroachments by the national government, curtailing the power of bureaucrats in general, and opposition to "big business" and to governmental policies that favor the interests of big business.

This is a program which in practice has not been able to compete effectively with the entrenched strength of the Liberal Democrats or with the mass prosperity that has characterized the Japanese economy since the late fifties, and for which the Liberal Democrats claim the credit.

The Japan Democratic Socialist Party (Nihon Minshu Shakaito)

In January, 1960, the heated dispute over both doctrinal and tactical issues that had long been seething below the surface of the Japan Socialist Party came to the boil. The party split in two, in a break of the sort that has been common among Japanese political parties of both the Left and the Right. On this occasion, the extreme right-wing faction of the party, led by Nishio Suehiro, plus a few members of the Kawakami Faction, walked out and established a party of its own known as the Japan Democratic Socialist Party. At the time, the dissidents had the support of some thirty-five Socialist members of the lower house of the National Diet, a number which increased to forty before the general election of November, 1960. They fared poorly in this election, however, and emerged with only seventeen seats, a drastic reduction in their parliamentary strength. They improved this holding to twenty-three seats in the 1963 general election and to thirty in the 1967 election but, despite this, their ultimate prospects remain uncertain.

The organization of the new party resembles that of the Socialist Party. At the head of the party is the chairman of its central executive committee, and a secretary-general is in charge of party administration. A party congress possesses ultimate authority and, in practice, the council composed of its members holding seats in the National Diet wields a good deal of influence. Since its members were for the most part experienced politicians to begin with, they individually and collectively had independent sources of financial support. In fact, during the 1960 and 1963 election campaigns, they were perhaps somewhat better off in this respect than were most of their former colleagues in the Socialist Party. In 1963 the party had a total declared income of 166,-029,000 yen ($461,000).

The Democratic Socialist's leadership differs in important respects from that of the Center and left-wing elements of the Socialist Party. It includes a higher percentage of former prefectural assemblymen and elective local officials and a somewhat smaller proportion of former union leaders and college graduates. Many of them are prewar Socialists of a slightly older generation. Their union associations are with *Domei*—that is, with a politically moderate labor federation rather than with the more radical *Sohyo* groups—and their backgrounds and experiences distinguish them rather sharply from their left-wing associates. In 1965 the Democratic Socialists claimed a party membership of 29,110.

The moderate and pragmatic socialism of the Democratic Socialist Party strives for a middle ground between the Liberal Democrats and the Socialists. Thus, while rejecting the policy of neutralism, the party advocates the gradual modification of the security treaty with the United States and the eventual withdrawal of American troops from Japanese soil; it favors also a foreign policy based on cooperation with the free world through the United Nations and a more cautious China policy than that of the Socialists. In 1965 the party chose to vote for the Korean treaty that was so bitterly opposed by the Socialists. Domestically, it places strong emphasis on the national or "mass" basis of socialism, as opposed to an exclusive working-class basis, advocates governmental aid in the development of low-cost housing projects, and the extension of cheap, governmentally-backed credit to small- and medium-sized industries and to farmers.

Its program thus represents a middle way, but some would say that it therefore has sacrificed drama, controversy, and the ability to influence a large number of voters. Whatever the reason, the party's candidates did poorly in the 1960 general election, and made only a modest recovery in 1963 and 1967. It remains to be seen whether or not this brand of moderate socialism can attract and hold the support of any sizable segment of the Japanese electorate.

The Japan Communist Party (Nihon Kyosanto)

The Communist Party has been a legal political party in Japan since General Douglas MacArthur released its leaders from prison in October, 1945. Although its top leaders went underground for a time during the Korean conflict, the party has run candidates in every general election since 1946. Its electoral and parliamentary successes have been modest. Normally, Communist candidates have polled between two and five per cent of the popular vote in a general election and have obtained from none to five of the lower house's 486 seats. The party does not, therefore, constitute a serious political force at the parliamentary level. It has no official influence on the determination of Japan's domestic or foreign policy. What political strength it has is exerted along other lines and, in particular, through its ability to infiltrate its members or sympathizers into positions of influence in particular unions or other organizations. This ability gives it a significant, but indirect, political strength.

The Japan Communist Party is probably the most tightly and effectively organized of any of Japan's political parties, although it has certainly not been free from factionalism and doctrinal strife. Ultimate authority within the party is theoretically vested in a party congress, but actually is wielded by shifting coalitions within the central committee. Recently the most prominent leaders have been Miyamoto Kenji, the party's secretary-general, and Hakamada Satomi, chief of its pro-Peking elements. The number of members in the party is difficult to ascertain with accuracy, because of its practice of maintaining both registered and nonregistered members. It was estimated to be about 130,000 in 1965. There are said to be some 200,000 subscribers to the daily and 900,000 to the Sunday editions of the party newspaper, *Akahata*. Its hard-core electoral support, that is, those who vote the Communist ticket in local as well as national elections, has never since the war reached one million in an electorate now numbering almost sixty million.

Since 1960 the Japan Communist Party, like all other Asian communist parties, has experienced severe internal strife as a result of the Sino-Soviet rift. By late 1963 it was apparent that the pro-Peking elements of the leadership had been victorious, and this was publicly confirmed by the formal expulsion from the party in 1964 of Shiga Yoshio and a number of other prominent pro-Soviet leaders. These purgees banded together in December, 1964, to form a small, separate, and pro-Soviet party known as the Japan Communist Party (Voice of Japan). By 1966, however, it became apparent that the internal unity and strength of the pro-Peking elements in the Japan Communist Party proper had waned and that the party was assuming a more neutral posture toward both Peking and Moscow.

The party's finances are something of a mystery. In 1963, for example, the party declared an income of 1,061,282,201 yen ($2,948,000) which made it on the record the second most affluent of all of the parties, with more than twice the admitted income of the far larger Socialist Party. Most of these funds doubtless derive from domestic sources, but it is persistently rumored that a considerable share of the party's income in recent years came from Peking.

The current party program advocates abrogation of the security treaty with the United States, the withdrawal of American forces from Japan, recognition of the Chinese People's Republic, friendship and closer relations with China, and a number of domestic measures calculated to improve the economic circumstances of the less well-off elements of the Japanese population. Its dominant theme, however, is anti-Americanism.

The Fair Play Party (Komeito)

Religious sects have not normally organized their own political parties in Japan, although there have been religious overtones to the programs of some of the right-wing or ultranationalist parties both before and since the war. The Fair Play Party is unusual, therefore, in the sense that it explicitly represents one of the so-called "new religions" of Japan, the *Sokagakkai*, or Value Creation Society. The faith was established by Makiguchi Tsunesaburo about 1930, ostensibly as an offshoot of the long-established *Nichiren* sect of Buddhism. It did not really achieve national importance until the mid-1950's, but today it is without a doubt the most energetic, militant, and widely discussed religious movement in Japan. It claims a membership of fifteen million, and even its critics are willing to grant it something in the neighborhood of ten.

Sokagakkai first entered politics in the Tokyo local elections of 1955 and succeeded in returning several of its members to seats on the prefectural and ward assemblies. In the upper house election of 1956, it elected three of its candidates to the House of Councillors. In 1959 five more of its members were elected to the upper house and 293 to various local assemblies throughout the country. These successes continued in the 1962 and 1965 House of Councillors' elections, with nine victories in the former and eleven in the latter. *Sokagakkai* is now the third largest party in the upper house.

In January, 1962, *Sokagakkai* established a separate political branch called the League for Fair Politics (*Komei Seiji Remmei*). In 1964 this was transformed into an official political party called the Fair Play Party (*Komeito*). The party ran a very effective campaign during the 1967 general election and returned twenty-five of its thirty-two candidates to the lower house. It seems to be adequately financed, having declared an income of 231,042,925 yen ($641,-700) during 1963, for example.

It is difficult to say just what the Fair Play Party stands for politically. Its leaders call themselves "neosocialists," but actually their statements and programs have little in common with orthodox Marxism. They advocate a renovation of society based on religious premises, the purification of politics, and a somewhat vague series of stands in favor of doubling welfare payments, abolishing the income tax, and conducting fair elections. They have also opposed rearmament for Japan, atomic testing, and the visits of American nuclear submarines to Japanese ports. In general, however, their policy statements have lacked specificity or coherence, a fact that so far at least, seems to have in no way diminished the party's electoral appeal.

However vague its program, a party that was able to poll more than five million votes—the third highest party total—in the national constituency sector of the 1965 House of Councillors election is obviously entitled to serious consideration. Its performance in the 1967 election for the lower house provided a better indication of the nature of the long-term threat that the Komeito poses to the established positions of the Liberal Democratic and Socialist Parties. Both are worried on this score and uncertain as to whether the new party will draw more votes from the ranks of former conservatives or of former socialist supporters. If they cannot crush this new contender, both of the older major parties would obviously like to ally it to their cause on as favorable terms as possible. If they fail in this endeavor and if the Fair Play Party is able over the next five to ten years to duplicate and sustain in the lower house its remarkable record of expanding strength in the upper house, it is conceivable that Japan may find itself possessed of three rather than two major political parties, with the Fair Play Party holding a casting vote between the conservatives and the progressives. This is still highly conjectural, however. Many practical politicians feel that the Fair Play Party really has no significant long-term role to play in Japanese politics.

General Characteristics of Japanese Parties

If we look at the general political party situation in Japan, several characteristics stand out. First, none of the parties—save perhaps the Fair Play Party—are truly mass membership organizations. They notably lack solid bases in popular involvement and support. They normally operate in Tokyo and among circles limited almost exclusively to professional politicians and administrators. They are essentially parliamentary parties. Their prime focus of interest is the lower house of the National Diet and what goes on there. Only during election campaigns do they engage in massive and sustained contact with the people. They are increasingly aware of the unsatisfactory nature and the dangers of this sort of relationship with the electorate and are seeking more meaningful forms of association. So far they do not seem to have found them. This is true of both conservative and progressive parties.

Second, both major parties are unstable and internally disunited. Both the Liberal Democrats and the Socialists are really congeries of factions held together primarily by the tactical requirements of effective campaigning and parliamentary competition. Within both parties there is a great deal of disagreement on major issues of policy and program. Where the Liberal Democrats are concerned, neither the party nor its several factions may be said really to have a basic program. The party's politics are pragmatic and professional rather than ideological. The Socialists, being primarily ideological in their orientation, share some common theoretical ground among themselves, but differ so fiercely over the all-important means of translating theory into practice that they are in fact at least as disunified as their opposition. Indeed, it seems to be easier for the practically oriented conservatives to reach agreements on particular political issues than for the more theoretically oriented progressives to do so. The results of such a situation are constant instability and strife within each party. The first concern of a party leader must be the careful nursing of the factional coalition which supports him in power; the loss of even one element may well be fatal to his leadership. These are not circumstances conducive to strong, continuous, or courageous party leadership. As a consequence, although the parties—or, more specifically, their leadership elements—do increasingly discuss and suggest national policies and formulate these as bills for parliamentary adoption, the policies concerned are almost certain to represent the end product of an elaborate series of compromises. Between the two major parties, the fundamental differences in their political orientation produce a marked and dangerous lack of common ground. A rigorous, theoretically oriented approach to politics confronts a hostile and pragmatically oriented approach. The terms and levels of discourse are different, and, on issues judged to be basic, both sides are inflexible. Pitched battles rather than parliamentary processes are frequently the result.

Finally, it should be clear that although the party situation since 1955 has resulted in the emergence of two major and competing political parties, Japan does not have a two-party system in our sense of the phrase. Only once since 1945, and then briefly, have the Socialists been able to form a Cabinet—and that a weak coalition. Under present circumstances, they do not have the votes or the parliamentary strength to come to power. They seem, temporarily at least, unable to raise the number of their seats in the lower house much beyond the one-third point. The result has been aptly described as a "one-and-a-half-party system," that is, a situation in which the Liberal Democrats, as long as they preserve some measure of party unity, are apt to remain in power and continue to provide the Cabinets which rule Japan, while the Socialists are consigned to the role of a more or less permanent, if not "loyal," opposition. It would, however, be risky to predict that such a condition will last indefinitely. It has been true since 1955, but we must remember that these have been years of unexampled prosperity and freedom from national crises in Japan. A drastic change in these circumstances could readily alter the "one-and-a-half-party system" and substitute some multiparty variant.

Political Interest Groups

As societies grow more complex and modern in their social, economic, and political characteristics, so, too, do the promotional and regulatory interests and activities of their governments expand. More and more individual and group actions are significantly affected by the decisions of legislators and bureaucrats, and as a consequence public interest in and involvement with government increase. In nontotalitarian societies, the public's desire and ability to influence such governmental decisions also increase. One way in which this is done is through the popular election of legislators to represent the interests and desires of their constituents in the decision-making process. But this alone is not adequate under modern circumstances. No one legislator can even begin to represent effectively the variety of urban, rural, industrial, commercial, financial, labor, women's, local, national, social, cultural, and other interests represented by a geographically defined constituency of several hundred thousand people. To fill this deficiency, interest groups provide a second level of representation and a more precisely focused means of representing the views and interests of a particular group to political parties, legislators, administrators, or the public. No society lacks some form of interest-group activity, but in pre-modern societies such activity is normally inclined to be more personalized, episodic, private, local, and diffuse, whereas in modern societies it is more apt to be systematically organized, relatively impersonal in style, continuous, public, and focused on larger targets.

Types of Interest Groups

Japan in the 1960's is rapidly approximating this "modern" sort of interest-group structure, although the pace of social change has been slower and more piecemeal in the countryside than in the cities. The farmers are more traditionally minded and usually more difficult to organize into interest groups than are city dwellers. The villages do not lack interest groups (for example, the almost universal and flourishing agricultural and irrigation cooperatives), but they are not nearly as common or conspicuous as in the cities. Most important among the nationally organized agricultural interest groups are probably the Japan Farmers' Union (*Nichino*), the National Federation of Agricultural Cooperative Purchasing Associations (*Zenkoren*), the National Federation of Agricultural Cooperative Marketing Associations (*Zenhanren*), a similar National Federation of Agricultural Cooperative Mutual Insurance Associations (*Kyosairen*), and the Japanese Forestry Association (*Nichirinkyo*). These are all postwar organizations, except the Japan Farmers' Union, which was founded in 1922 and has a long history of struggle for the rights of tenants and small farmers against landlord interests; it has also had close connections with a variety of socialist causes and parties.

The several national federations of agricultural cooperatives were formed mainly as a means of securing favorable consideration from the government for the economic interests which they represent. They regularly engage in lobbying and other forms of political pressure. One of them has been charged with outright bribery of officials in the Ministry of Agriculture and Forestry. Another type of interest group that might be added to this list is local and rural though not specifically agricultural in character: the National Association of Towns and Villages (*Zenkoku Chosonkai*) or the National Association of Chairmen of Town and Village Assemblies (*Zenkoku Chosongikai Gichokai*). There are similar organizations at the city and prefectural levels. A significant part of their activity is also devoted to the representation of local interests before the national government, particularly in the fields of subsidies and grants-in-aid. In general, however, such formal and systematically organized interest groups are a recent addition to the rural scene in Japan. Their relations to the average farmer are still largely tenuous, and the countryside is still notable more for the absence than for the presence of modern interest-group activities.

The cities of Japan present a completely different picture. Systematically organized groups with well-defined political interests and programs flourish. Take, as a fairly typical example, the Minami District of Osaka City. The District Office issues annually a directory of organizations within its boundaries that in some way direct their activities toward the public. It takes seventy closely printed pages in a recent edition simply to list the names and top officers of these groups and their branches. The entire city may in this way be viewed as a web of such groups organized along both geographical lines (for example, by shopping districts, streets, or blocks) and functional lines (by industry, trade, or specific interest). Particularly active in local, and sometimes in national, politics are such groups as the Red Cross Service Organization (*Nisseki Hoshidan*), the Federation of Housewives (*Shufuren*), the League of War Widows (*Mibojinkai*), and many others. A list of this sort could be prolonged indefinitely.

The really major operators, however, are the representatives of organized business and organized labor. Most active politically among the business contingent are the Japanese Federation of Employers' Organizations (*Nikkeiren*) and the Japanese Political League of Small and Medium Enterprises (*Chuseiren*). The first of these is an association of employers' associations and represents more than twenty thousand of Japan's largest employers. It frequently propagandizes the government and the public on policies affecting business and labor relations, and is said to serve as a means of communication between business interests and the conservative parties. It is widely regarded as one of the most influential pressure groups in Japan. The Political League of Small and Medium Enterprises attempts to play a similar role on behalf of this seriously depressed segment of the Japanese economy. It works in particular for tax relief and expanded credit facilities for its members. Other national business organizations, such as the Federation of Economic Organizations (*Keidanren*) and the Japanese Management Association (*Doyukai*), also work politically and patently on behalf of business interests. Collectively, these business associations provide much of the financial support for the Liberal Democratic Party and its electoral campaigns and candidates.

The General Council of Japanese Labor Unions (*Sohyo*) is by far the most active and powerful of labor's interest groups. A federation of unions with more than four million members representing approximately forty-five per cent of the total number of unionized workers in Japan, its interests are more political than economic. It is the mainstay of the Japan Socialist Party in both electoral and financial terms, and has taken an extremely strong and aggressive stand in favor of neutralism and closer relations with Peking and Moscow, and against the mutual security treaty with the United States, American bases in Japan, atomic weapons, increases in the power of the police, and all conservative Cabinets. It also regularly nominates and backs candidates in election campaigns. In the 1963 general election, for example, about forty per cent of the Socialist Party's successful candidates were sponsored by unions that for the most part were members of *Sohyo*. Its normal policy might be described as left-wing Socialist, though this has somewhat moderated recently.

Sohyo's major rival as a labor interest group is a second federation of unions known as the All-Japan Labor Federation (*Domei*), which represents about 1.8 million members. Its interests are more centered on economic matters and are thus less political than *Sohyo*'s. Being closely linked with the Democratic Socialist Party, however, it favors a more moderate brand of socialism. In addition to these two major federations, certain individual unions and associations also maintain very active political interests and programs. The Japan Teachers' Union (*Nikkyoso*) and the National Federation of Students' Self-Government Associations (*Zengakuren*), for example, have campaigned constantly, and sometimes violently, for a variety of political causes espoused by the Socialist and Communist Parties.

Interest Groups in Politics

Japan thus has a large and increasing complement of interest groups. Our knowledge of their structure and activities still leaves a good deal to be desired, but the following generalizations might be ventured. At both the national and local levels, the majority of them seem to be involved in politics. Their involvement is of at least two different types. The first is electoral in nature, stemming from the fact that the secret of success at the polls lies in skillfully appealing to units or blocks of voters and in garnering adequate financial support. To the practical politician, an interest group represents primarily a potential and accessible bloc of votes plus a source of campaign contributions. Many interest groups, on their part, are not loathe to play such a political role for selected politicians in return for preferred access to his attention and influence once he is in office. In one arena or another, then, the average Japanese interest group does support candidates for election to local or national office.

How effective such support is we do not know in general, but in particular cases it is quite obvious that certain members of the National Diet owe their seats almost entirely to the support of certain interest groups. A recent study concludes that fifty-nine of the 467 members elected to the lower house in 1963 were, in effect, there primarily as the representatives of particular unions —fourteen for *Nikkyoso* (the Japan Teachers' Union) alone, for example. This practice, of course, represents an extreme variant of the more normal situation in which a given interest group is simply one of many groups supporting a particular candidate. In the case of these labor unions, they in effect constitute themselves as a sort of *ad hoc* political party and support their own candidates for office.

The second type of interest-group political action is directed toward particular political figures, primarily high-level administrators. In Japan, the relations between the Ministries and high administrative offices of the national government and their organized public clienteles are apt to be very close, for example, between the Ministry of Agriculture and Forestry and the organized farm groups throughout Japan, or between the Ministry of International Trade and Industry and the organized business groups which it ostensibly regulates. In fact, the Ministry, to simplify its administrative relationships with such clientele groups, is sometimes responsible for their establishment in organized form to begin with. The resultant relationship is complex. Once in existence, such an organization will perform the functions of a political interest or pressure group, but its representations will be made to a group of officials in Tokyo with whom it maintains the closest and most cordial relationships. This is particularly true of interest groups of a business, agricultural, technical, or professional nature. Labor unions and left-wing affiliated interest groups are apt to have more difficult problems of access.

As an outgrowth of this sort of relationship, however, the interest groups commonly provide important—and sometimes sinecure—positions for the high officials of their particular Ministry, when these men choose to retire from governmental service, normally about the age of fifty. The retired and experienced bureaucrat then becomes a leading employee of the interest which he formerly regulated and serviced and, at the same time, its representative in charge of negotiations with the Ministry, office, or bureau which he formerly headed. It is often claimed that arrangements for such positions are made clandestinely before the bureaucrat's retirement and that he consequently becomes an undercover agent within the government for the interest group involved. A good deal of administrative corruption is alleged to result from such practices. Not infrequently, such former bureaucrats also proceed to organize local political support for themselves on the basis of their interest-group affiliations and to run for national elective office, particularly in the House of Councillors.

The political targets of most Japanese interest groups have traditionally been the government administration rather than the legislature. The reason is simple. Executives and bureaucrats, rather than legislators, have made most of the important decisions in Japanese politics and administration, or, if they have not made them, they have at least interpreted and applied them, which is apt to be of equal importance. Since the war, as the political role of the House of Representatives has gradually increased in importance, interest groups are perhaps paying greater attention to the legislature and its committees, but their stress remains heavily on the higher bureaucracy. Members of the legislature still seem to serve primarily as intermediaries between interest-group representatives from their constituencies and high officials of the national government and, perhaps to some degree, as a means of bringing favorable budgetary or other pressures to bear on such officials.

We lack extensive or reliable information about the predominant style of Japanese interest-group activities before bureaucrats and legislators. The press is largely convinced that in many cases the lobbies depend heavily on corrupt and illegal techniques. Public trials and investigations have demonstrated the truth of such claims in specific cases, but we lack the evidence to generalize about more serious forms of bribery and corruption. Quite obviously, the minor corruptions represented by *geisha* parties, elegant meals, and expensive entertainment for strategically placed individuals flourish in Tokyo as in other capitals. Equally obvious, and perhaps more serious, is the practice of providing positions for retired bureaucrats. There does seem to be a tendency, however, for some of the major Japanese interest groups to place increasing emphasis on "educational materials" and appeals for broad popular support. These might forecast some sort of shift away from the older and more personalized techniques of influence.

Political interest groups have definitely established a firm and expanding role for themselves in the Japanese political system. On balance, they have almost certainly enabled many interests to have more effective representation before the government. They have probably advanced, if largely inadvertently, the cause of more popular and responsible government in Japan. Indeed, the degree to which they flourish today is one of the basic factors distinguishing the postwar from the prewar political scene in Japan. More needs to be done, however, to give all interest groups equal access to the government, for at present some groups undoubtedly get preferential treatment. To a certain degree this is inevitable in a party system of government, but if some interest groups are denied access to the government, the long-term political consequences might be very serious.

Political Leadership

The characteristics and quality of political leadership in postwar Japan are particularly difficult to assess. As we have seen, both Japanese tradition and practice place far less emphasis on individual "leaders" and "leadership" than does our own culture. This tendency is reinforced by the multifactional nature of political party leadership and the prevalence of committee and consensual techniques of decision making. Under such circumstances, it becomes peculiarly difficult to assign meaningful responsibility for particular political policies or actions and thus to determine what any given "leader" may have contributed to a particular decision. Despite such problems, we can, of course, still identify certain persons who occupy positions of leadership in the Japanese political system. Among these, we have already described the members of the Liberal Democratic and Socialist contingents in the House of Representatives. Let us now look at a still more selective and important leadership group, the Cabinet, which represents the top level of politically conservative leadership. The characteristics of the top socialist leadership do not vary notably from those of the party's Diet delegation described earlier.

An examination of appointments to recent conservative Cabinets will demonstrate the impact of war, defeat, and the American Occupation on the nature of Japan's political leadership. The military figures and the representatives of court circles and the aristocracy so prominent before the war are no longer encountered. Among the prewar elites, only the party politicians, the bureaucrats, and the representatives of business have survived. The onus of defeat, the American-enforced purge of military and ultranationalist elements from public office, and the provisions of the new Constitution combined to drive the traditional leaders from office; in the resulting vacuum of leadership, new faces—or at least new looks—appeared in the higher ranks of the conservative parties and for the most part remain there today.

The standing of these leaders is not based on their appeal to the masses. Just as Japan's political parties are largely associations of professional politicians rather than mass membership organizations, so too are the ranks of her leaders filled by private and closeted means rather than by any sort of popularity contest. In conservative circles, it makes very little difference whether a given person is an accomplished public speaker or possessed of a personality with wide popular appeal. The meaningful criteria are more apt to be length of political service, abilities as a fund raiser, skill as a tactician, administrative ability, possession of useful connections, and a personal reputation for loyalty and sincerity. Such a system tends to bring to the fore men of experience, caution, and a generally conservative approach to political problems rather than more brilliant or venturesome types. Almost all the conservative leaders have had long experience in government. Article 68 of the Constitution requires that a majority of the Ministers of State, that is, the Cabinet, must be chosen from among the members of the Diet, and custom decrees that a large majority hold seats in the lower house during their Cabinet service. From 1946 to 1960 seventy-nine per cent of the Cabinet held seats in the lower house, and twenty per cent were members of the upper house. Cabinet appointments from outside the membership of the National Diet are thus very rare, almost never amounting to more than one or two in a given Cabinet.

Reliable information about the members of recent conservative Cabinets is not readily available. The published data leave much to be desired. A survey of the initial membership of the nine Cabinets holding office between 1954 and 1961, however, yields some relevant information. The average age of the group upon taking office has been just under sixty, with a range running from thirty-nine to seventy-eight. The Prime Ministers themselves have had an average age of sixty-two, with Mr. Ishibashi, at seventy-two, being by far the oldest and Mr. Kishi, at sixty, the youngest. During this period, only one woman was appointed to Cabinet office, a post which she held for less than five months. The educational level of the ministers was uniformly high. Of the some 153 posts involved, only two were filled by persons who were not graduates of a university, college, or higher commercial, technical, or normal school. Among the schools concerned, Tokyo University, and especially its Law School, was predominant. Sixty-two ministerial posts—some forty-one per cent of the total—were filled by the graduates of this single university. The universities with the next highest numbers were Waseda and Kyoto, each of which had approximately fourteen per cent of the total.

A comparable analysis of the career backgrounds of Cabinet Ministers is more difficult. All the persons we are examining are, at this stage of their careers, primarily politicians. Their earlier careers are harder to characterize. Many have had several different types of employment and have combined these with political activities in varying proportions. Judgments about the dominant strain in a man's professional background will, therefore, differ and the same individual is apt to be counted in more than a single category. One such survey of Cabinets between 1946 and 1960 concludes that about thirty per cent of those holding ministerial posts have had primarily bureaucratic backgrounds as career members of the national civil service, that another sixteen per cent might best be characterized as local politicians, while forty per cent came from the ranks of business, twelve per cent had once been lawyers, and another eleven per cent were former journalists. These figures make plausible one formula for political success commonly advanced in postwar Japan, that is, that the path to the top leads from *Ichiko,* Tokyo's famous First Higher School, through the Law Department of Tokyo University, into the higher ranks of the national bureaucracy, and thence to the Cabinet. The relative prevalence of both Tokyo University graduates and ex-bureaucrats in recent Cabinets lends considerable force to such a claim. In fact, the bureaucratic and, allegedly, undemocratic background of so many Cabinet Ministers is perhaps the most common and bitter complaint against recent political leadership encountered in Japanese circles today.

Another important aspect of Japanese Cabinets is the fact that the rate of turnover is very high. The average life of a Cabinet since the surrender has been only about nine and a half months, and new Cabinets usually mean new faces. Only Prime Ministers and, occasionally, Foreign Ministers show any degree of greater longevity within the Cabinet. The Prime Minister is, in fact, under constant and strenuous pressure to rotate his Cabinet as rapidly as possible to accommodate an endless chain of the politically deserving. Ministerial status is widely regarded as the *summum bonum* of political life in Japan, and a successful Prime Minister, to preserve his own position, must spread these offices as widely as possible.

We now come to a deeper truth about political leadership in Japan. Since this merry-go-round of Ministers cannot readily hold the reins of power, political leadership actually resides with the Prime Minister, the leaders of the several factions in the majority party, the somewhat more stable membership of the higher ranks of the professional bureaucracy, and the business leaders who finance the Liberal Democratic Party. The backgrounds of these men are essentially like those already described for the Cabinet. Perhaps the most interesting thing about them is their relative lack of conspicuousness. Only the Prime Minister stands forth prominently above the turbulent political waters. The factional leaders and the top bureaucrats operate largely below the surface. And below them lie still deeper levels of politicians, bureaucrats, and businessmen, whose range of influence remains largely conjectural. This covert and collective nature of the present political leadership in Japan, however, reflects one of the country's most venerable and traditional political characteristics. Throughout Japanese history, the people actually wielding political power have seldom been visible. They have usually been found in shifting combinations of groups and individuals lying several strata below the surface institutions of politics. The present combination of both visible power and real power in the person of the Prime Minister therefore represents a partial departure from the traditional arrangements.

Chapter *7*

Decision Making

THE ORGANS OF
GOVERNMENT

The primary function of politics is to enable men to make and administer decisions in the realm of public affairs, an area which is variously defined by different societies. The machinery by which these decisions are formally made and administered is called *government*. Government provides both a mechanism for determining and administering public policies, and a process for bestowing legitimacy on the decisions and products of this mechanism. In practice, it does more than this; by providing a context and a structure for the making of official decisions, it also in time comes to influence the types of questions that are posed and of decisions that are made. Government—the formal political institutions of a society—thus interacts continuously with the broader and less formalized "political system" or "political process" of a given society.

The political system includes government, but also encompasses such unofficial components of a society's decision-making apparatus as interest groups, the leadership structure, value systems, political style, and so forth. Since the government and the political system are intimately linked and vitally affect each other, there is a constant struggle among interests and groups for control of some or all of the mechanisms of government. Whoever controls government controls the official apparatus for promulgating his views and promoting his interests and thus has a distinct advantage over his competitors. When reading the following exposition of the organization and functions of the Japanese government, keep in mind the stakes involved. Control of the machinery of government is the immediate issue in the political struggle in Japan. This machinery is the instrument of political achievement.

The Constitution of Japan

Politics involves struggle and competition, and, to keep these within tolerable limits, societies agree on certain rules to regulate the game of politics. Some of these rules are adjudged to be more fundamental than others and are usually formulated into separate bodies of law known as constitutions. These regulations command greater status and veneration, are presumed to have more permanency, and are deliberately made harder to change than the normal body of laws and ordinances.

Japan has in modern times had two constitutions. The first of these, usually known as the Meiji Constitution, was promulgated in 1889 and took effect in 1890. The second, known simply as the Constitution of Japan, was promulgated on November 3, 1946, and took effect six months later on May 3, 1947. Its origins were most unusual. These were the early days of the Allied Occupation, and General MacArthur, the Supreme Commander for the Allied Powers (SCAP), had, in effect, been charged with the democratization of Japan. The higher American officials involved in the Occupation generally agreed that the achievement of this goal would necessitate some rather substantial changes in the Meiji Constitution. The Japanese government was so informed, and, during the early months of the Occupation, the initiative was left in its hands. However, when by February, 1946, the committee established by the Japanese Cabinet to propose revisions in the Meiji Constitution showed no signs of recommending the types of democratic changes judged necessary by General MacArthur and his aides, the entire matter was secretly turned over to SCAP's Government Section, which was ordered to produce a model constitution incorporating the types of political changes General MacArthur considered necessary.

The decision to intervene directly and decisively at this time in the rewriting of the Japanese Constitution was probably due to the fact that the Far Eastern Commission, an international agency responsible for setting basic policies for the Allied Occupation of Japan, was scheduled to commence its activities in Washington on February 26, 1946. If the United States, or any of its agents such as SCAP, was interested in having a controlling voice in the contents of a new Japanese constitution, it was essential that it act before February 26. In fact, the decision to do so at this particular time seems to have been taken solely on General MacArthur's own authority in Tokyo, and the authorities in Washington appear to have known nothing about it until the first draft of the new Constitution was published in Japan on March 6, 1946.

In six days, between February 4 and 10, the Government Section produced, in English, the original draft of the present Japanese Constitution. This draft was first submitted to the Japanese at a small private meeting on February 13. During the nine days which followed, the draft was translated into Japanese, and sufficient pressure was brought upon the Japanese Cabinet to insure its reluctant adoption of this draft as its own. Thereafter, the Cabinet Draft—as it was now known—went through several revisions which resulted in some changes, largely minor in nature, after which it was submitted to the Imperial Diet as a proposal for the total amendment of the Meiji Constitution. After extensive debate, especially in the House of Peers, the bill of amendment was adopted by overwhelming majorities in both houses and subsequently promulgated by the Emperor. The circumstances were such that any other form of action by the Japanese was almost inconceivable. In this fashion, the present Constitution was drafted and put into effect.

The new Constitution, although almost twice as long as the Meiji Constitution, is reasonably brief as modern constitutions go—it consists of a preamble, 11 chapters, and 103 articles. The Constitution provides a system of government based essentially on a unique amalgam of British and American institutions (Fig. 7-1). It preserves the monarchy, but strips the Emperor of any semblance of political authority. It also retains a bicameral legislature, but completely reconstitutes the relationship and powers of the prewar upper and lower houses. Superior legislative and financial powers are entrusted to the lower house. At the national level, executive and administrative authority is concentrated in a responsible Cabinet, and an independent American-style judiciary is vested with the power of judicial review. The Constitution places great stress on civil rights and includes what is probably one of the world's most detailed and ambitious constitutional statements of the rights and duties of the people. It further introduces into Japanese law for the first time the principle of local autonomy, involving decentralization of national power and a reciprocal increase in the rights and independence of local governments to a degree quite foreign to earlier Japanese practice.

One of the best-known and most controversial provisions of the Constitution appears in Chapter II, Article 9, the famous "renunciation of war" clause, whereby Japan renounces war as a sovereign right of the nation and the threat or use of force as a means of settling international disputes. Indeed, the Con-

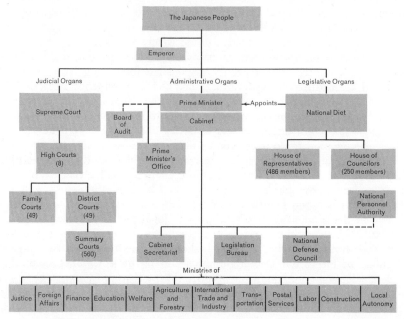

- - - - - - - Indicates semi-autonomous status or indirect control

FIGURE 7-1. THE ORGANIZATION OF JAPAN'S NATIONAL GOVERNMENT. *(Adapted from* Shokuinroku, *1966, Vol. I.)*

stitution seems to obligate Japan never to maintain land, sea, or air forces. This is the only known instance in which a major modern state constitutionally renounces war. The Constitution also specifically provides that it is the supreme law of the land, and that no act contrary to its provisions shall have legal force or validity. Amendments to the Constitution require initiation by a two-thirds concurring vote of all members of both houses of the National Diet and ratification by the people through an affirmative vote by a majority of those participating in a referendum on the proposed amendment.

Taken all in all, this is an admirably democratic constitution. It introduces democratic rights, institutions, and practices into Japanese politics that undoubtedly go far beyond anything the Japanese themselves might realistically have been expected to establish, had they been left to their own devices. In fact, on the basis of text alone, it is a considerably more democratic document than is the Constitution of the United States. The Constitution is also a workable document, although it has flaws and does create problems. For example, any pronounced degree of local autonomy is probably impractical in Japan, judicial review has not proven particularly meaningful in practice, and some of the more ambitious civil and human rights and freedoms envisaged in Chapter III of the Constitution will probably long remain pious hopes rather than social or legal facts. On the other hand, the Diet, the Cabinet, the judiciary, and the bureaucracy are functioning with surprising efficiency along the general lines envisaged in the Constitution, and the country, operating under the Constitution, has successfully coped with most of its more pressing problems since 1947. Despite strong pressure from the conservative leadership to revise it in whole or part, the Constitution reads today as it did in 1947. No government has yet had the courage or the strength to launch an all-out campaign for its amendment. The fact that the 1947 Constitution stands unchanged, given its antecedents and the enormous political changes it imposed on a reluctant Japanese leadership, is perhaps the most remarkable phenomenon of all. The Japanese have adopted a new and largely foreign set of political institutions with surprising ease and speed, and have so far displayed a considerable reluctance to exchange them for something more familiar and more Japanese.

Despite its lack of success to date, however, a strong revisionist sentiment continues to flourish among some leaders of the Liberal Democratic Party. They argue that the present Constitution does not really represent the "freely expressed will of the Japanese people," that it was imposed by foreigners, that it is un-Japanese in both spirit and language, that it is poorly drafted, and that it needs changes in a number of particulars. Specifically, many of those who favor constitutional revision advocate such matters as a redefinition of the status of the Emperor, constitutional recognition of Japan's right of self-defense, some greater measure of limitation on individual rights when they conflict with the public interest, reforms in the composition and powers of the House of Councillors, the establishment of a special court to judge questions of constitutionality, an increase in the authority of the central government over the localities, and some easier system of constitutional amendment. None of these proposals tampers with the principle of popular sovereignty and none of them advocates—openly at least—any sort of across-the-board return to prewar conditions. Most of the proposals are for fairly moderate reforms. An officially appointed Commission on the Constitution, after some seven years of study, turned in a report in 1964 in which a large majority of its members recommended some measure of constitutional revision. Despite this, no actual amendments have yet been formally proposed, and it seems unlikely that the government will seriously attempt to press this issue in the near future.

Finally, it should be noted that not all the basic rules of Japanese politics are contained in the Constitution, which is supplemented in practice by a considerable number of basic laws. These put flesh onto the rather bare bones of the Constitution and prescribe the actual nature and operations of the country's primary political institutions. Examples of such laws are: the Imperial House Law, the National Diet Law, the Law of the Courts, the Cabinet Law, the Finance Law, the Public Office Election Law, and the Local Autonomy Law. Since these can be changed by normal statutes rather than by constitutional amendments, they add a desirable quality of flexibility to the structure of the state.

The Emperor

As we have seen, in postwar Japan the Emperor has only a symbolic role in the Japanese political system. The Emperor does not have any specifically political or executive functions of more than ritual or ceremonial importance. In the words of Article 1 of the Constitution:

> The Emperor shall be the symbol of the state and of the unity
> of the people, deriving his position from the will of the people
> with whom resides sovereign power.

The effect of this and the remaining articles of Chapter I is to deny the Emperor any "powers related to government" and to confine his official acts to such ceremonial functions as appointing the Prime Minister and Chief Judge of the Supreme Court (after they are designated by the Cabinet); promulgating laws, Cabinet orders, treaties, and amendments to the Constitution; convoking the Diet and dissolving the House of Representatives; attesting certain official appointments; awarding honors; receiving ambassadors and ministers; and performing certain other ceremonial functions. None of these involves any initiative, discretion, or influence on his part; he acts only at the behest of responsible governmental officials and in accordance with their decisions.

The Emperor is systematically informed about affairs of state and official policies, but his opinion about them is not formally solicited. Conceivably, on a few issues affecting the Imperial Family or in a moment of national crisis such as that posed in August, 1945, over the question of Japan's surrender—in which he did play a positive and critical role—the Emperor could exert influence, but this would be purely a function of his personal and institutional prestige. He has no legal or theoretical right to do so, and thus his official position is far weaker than that of the British monarch. Technically, he is not even "chief of state," but merely a "symbol of the state," a phrase which the conservative advocates of constitutional revision would like to change. Under these circumstances, the danger that the Emperor will once again become an effective screen for or political instrument of a revived militarist or ultranationalist faction seems remote.

The composition of the Imperial Family is rigidly and narrowly defined by law. It is limited to the legitimate and direct descendants of an Emperor. Adoption is not permitted within the Imperial Family. At present, the Imperial Family consists only of the reigning Emperor and his family plus the families of his three brothers. Succession to the throne is by the eldest son of the Emperor, followed by the eldest son of the eldest son. Matters of succession and regency are regulated by an Imperial House Council, which is completely controlled by ex officio members representing popularly responsible representatives of the legislature, the Cabinet, and the Supreme Court. Before the war, the Imperial Family was extremely wealthy in its own name; its critics, in fact, sometimes referred to it as "the greatest of the *zaibatsu* (cartels)." Since 1947, it has been stripped of most of its extensive holdings, save for personal property, and is supported primarily by sums voted annually by the National Diet—in 1965 it appropriated 647,354,000 yen ($1,798,205) to cover the expenses of the privy purse, the Imperial Family, and the Imperial household, plus an additional 3,270,099,000 yen ($9,083,603) to pay part of the construction costs of a new Imperial palace.

It would be a serious mistake to conclude that because of his purely ceremonial position and negligible governmental powers the Emperor does not play a very important role in the Japanese political system. A nation needs powerful, loyalty-begetting symbols about which to forge its national unity. The absence of such a nationally shared emotional rallying point is one of the greatest problems confronting many of the new states of Asia and Africa. For Japan, such a focus is provided pre-eminently by the Imperial Family. It symbolizes two thousand years of "Japaneseness," of the unity of the people and their culture. Under present circumstances, there is nothing that can readily or effectively take its place. Its role is not to be discounted nor lightly discarded, and many thoughtful Japanese are, therefore, understandably troubled by the low regard in which the Imperial institution is held by important segments of Japanese youth.

The National Legislature

The Constitution describes the Diet, or Parliament, of Japan as "the highest organ of state power" and "the sole law-making organ of the State." It further states that the Diet shall consist of two houses, a House of Representatives (or lower house) and a House of Councillors (or upper house). These provisions are basic, and their significance becomes most apparent when we compare them with the comparable clauses of the Meiji Constitution. Under the terms of that document, the Emperor was more than the highest organ of state power; in a mystical way, he embodied the state and wielded its sovereign powers. And although laws, formally, were the product of the Imperial Diet, both the Emperor and the Cabinet had the power to issue decrees which had the force of law. The present Constitution vests sovereignty in the people and makes the Diet both the highest organ of the people's sovereignty and the sole source of law. These changes are basic to both the legal and the power structure of the Japanese state. The government has thus been transformed from an Emperor-centered to a parliament-centered mechanism, and the elected representatives of the people have become vastly more powerful.

The organization and powers of the two houses of the Diet differ considerably. The House of Representatives is a body of 486 members who are returned from 123 districts by an electoral system that has already been described. Its members are, in theory, elected for four-year terms, but in practice no postwar Diet has survived that long without dissolution by the Cabinet. Actual terms between general elections have ranged from six and one-half months to three years and eight months. The tenure of members is thus indeterminate, and depends in practice on the relationship between the lower house and the Cabinet as well as on the internal political situation of the lower house.

The organization of the House of Representatives is quite simple. A Speaker, normally chosen from the ranks of the majority party, presides over its deliberations and maintains order. There is also a Vice-Speaker, who is frequently selected from among the membership of the opposition party. For deliberative purposes, the House functions either in plenary session or in committees. Under American influence, the latter have become the more important mode of operation. In 1966, there were some sixteen standing committees, with functions largely paralleling the principal divisions of the government's administrative organization, for example, foreign affairs, finance, justice, education, agriculture, local administration, budget, audit, etc. A Diet Operations Committee and a Committee on Discipline deal with problems of internal housekeeping. Members are assigned to these committees, and their chairmanships are allocated in accordance with the relative party strengths in the House. Assignments are actually made by the parties. Special committees also exist on a temporary basis to deal with particular problems. The members each have a private secretary provided at public expense, and the House as a whole is serviced by an administrative and custodial staff numbering 1,680 in 1965. The majority of these are organized into a Secretariat and a Bureau of Legislation. The National Diet Library also supplies reference and legislative services to the members of both houses.

The upper house, or House of Councillors, is constituted along somewhat different lines. Originally, the American Occupation authorities favored a unicameral legislature, and the first draft of the Constitution was written in this fashion. The Japanese leadership objected strenuously to this proposal, however, and favored an appointive upper house or a corporative one representing the professions and selected portions of the electorate. The present House of Councillors represents a somewhat unsatisfactory compromise between these two viewpoints. It consists of 250 members popularly elected from two different types of constituencies. One hundred and fifty are chosen from forty-six electoral districts—collectively called local constituencies—which are coterminous with the prefectures. The number of seats controlled by any one prefecture is roughly proportional to its population and varies from two for the smallest to eight each for Tokyo and Hokkaido. The remaining hundred members are chosen from the national constituency, which is to say that all Japan is regarded as a single electoral district where these members are concerned.

The terms of members are set at six years, and, since the upper house cannot be dissolved, its members usually serve the full period. Terms are staggered, however, and in practice one-half the membership in the categories described above is chosen at elections held at regular three-year intervals. In such elections, each elector votes twice, once for a candidate running in his local constituency and once for a candidate running in the national constituency. The justification advanced for this unusual and complicated system is that it combines the advantages of informed local representation with those of a panel of nationally eminent candidates. It has not actually worked out in this fashion, however. Although some men of truly national stature are elected from the national constituency, most of those so chosen probably represent organizations having branches or influence in several heavily populated areas of Japan, for example, labor unions, big business, and nationally organized interest groups. Under these circumstances, it is hardly surprising to find that the upper house has become practically as partisan a body as the lower house. Few independents are elected to either body; the great majority of the successful candidates run as party nominees. The party composition of the upper house closely resembles that of the lower, with the Liberal Democrats and independent conservatives controlling in recent years about three-fifths of the total membership and the combined progressive forces about one-third. The internal organization of the upper house closely parallels that already described for the lower house.

The relations between the upper and lower houses of the Diet are prescribed by both law and the Constitution, which combine to make the House of Representatives far stronger than the House of Councillors. For example, the lower house may enact a law against the opposition of the upper house by passing it a second time by a majority of two-thirds or more of the members present. Normally, however, legislative differences between the two houses are resolved by an interhouse conference committee. Again, on such important matters as the enactment of the budget, the selection of the Prime Minister, or the ratification of treaties, the House of Representatives can, against the Councillors' opposition, decide the issue by a simple majority vote. As a consequence, the legislative and political roles of the upper house have been distinctly subordinate to those of the lower house in both law and practice. Serious disagreements between the two houses do not often occur, however, and bills are normally processed by both without recourse to the above expedients. Under these circumstances, some Japanese feel that the upper house, as presently constituted, makes little if any positive contribution to the political process. This has led in recent years to arguments for its reform or reconstitution, particularly along corporative lines—that is, by having it be composed of representatives of the professions and other elements of the electorate.

The operations of this bicameral legislature are too complicated to admit of more than summary treatment. Its principal function is, in theory, the making of laws. It is, the Constitution says, the sole law-making organ of the state. In practice, however, few laws of any significance originate in either house of the Diet. The vast majority are initiated and drafted in bill form by bureaucrats serving in the Ministries and other administrative branches of the government. Some originate with the Cabinet, and some are initiated by the policy research committees of the political parties, which often work in collaboration with civil servants experienced in the field concerned. A recent survey of the 2,646 bills enacted into law by the 14th to 49th Diets (1951–1965) showed that 2,231 (84 per cent) were public bills, that is, they were introduced into the Diet and officially sponsored by the Cabinet, whereas only 415 (16 per cent) were private, or members', bills, and of these many were actually initiated and drafted by bureaucrats or party sources and turned over to an individual Diet member for sponsorship and formal introduction.

In fact, therefore, the Diet and its members do not actually make many laws. They take projects of law originating elsewhere and then examine, debate, and publicize them; sometimes they amend them, and eventually they enact many of them into law. This is not much different from what other major legislative bodies actually do in most Western democracies. In this system, the most important legislative deliberations and decisions take place in the standing committees; plenary sessions usually just ratify such prior committee decisions. Party discipline is exceedingly strict on legislative matters, and the members of any given party almost always vote as a solid bloc in committee and in the Diet. Given the so-called "one-and-one-half-party system" with its strong Liberal Democratic majorities in both houses, therefore, there is seldom any doubt as to the fate of a bill once it has been brought to a vote. The opposition is very skillful in the use of obstructionist techniques, however, and the real problem is often how to bring a proposal to a decisive vote without completely disrupting normal parliamentary procedures and relationships.

The Diet has other important functions in addition to legislation. Japan has a parliamentary system of government in most respects, and the Prime Minister must be selected from among the members of the Diet—in practice, from the lower house—by a formal resolution of the Diet. The House of Representatives alone has the right to vote lack of confidence in the Cabinet and thus to bring about either its resignation or a dissolution of the House and a general election. The Constitution also entrusts the ultimate and sole authority to raise and spend money for public purposes to the Diet. All taxes that are levied and all payments from public funds must be authorized by law. Both of these activities are provided for annually in the national budget bill and its several supplements. These constitute the government's over-all income and expenditure plan for the year. Budget bills must be submitted first to the House of Representatives, where they receive the most extensive and careful of scrutinies. Probably no regular activity of the Diet is considered to be of more importance than its approval of the budget. Strangely enough by American standards, the houses usually attempt to raise rather than cut the estimated expenditures approved by the Cabinet. The Diet is also responsible for approving the government's settled accounts. An independent Board of Audit examines these for accuracy and legality, and its report must finally be examined and accepted by the Diet. Finally, both houses of the Diet have been given investigative functions by the new Constitution. They are empowered to appoint special committees which can call and hear witnesses and demand records in matters relating to the efficiency or honesty of government. The Diet in this way is supposed to exercise a continuing supervisory function over the quality of governmental performance.

This legal and organizational description of the National Diet does not, however, convey an adequate picture of its actual operations and its role in the larger political system. It has several other characteristics which should be noted. First, its internal political alignments reflect, of course, the relative strengths of the various political parties. The government party, currently the Liberal Democrats, controls about three-fifths of the seats in both houses through the unremitting application of a rigorous system of party discipline over its Diet members. As a consequence, it can dominate proceedings both in committees and on the floor whenever it is willing to pay the price of doing so. The Socialist opposition parties are thus relegated to the difficult and trying position of a seemingly permanent minority. This creates very serious strains on normal parliamentary procedure. The dilemma for members of the opposition is this: What should they do when the government party attempts to enact a piece of legislation which runs directly counter to what they consider to be the vital interests of their party or the Japanese people? Their chance of coming to power themselves by normal electoral means seems small in the foreseeable future. Should they then abide by normal parliamentary practice and allow the Liberal Democratic majority to pass the legislation in question, or should they have recourse to filibustering and obstructionist tactics, climaxed perhaps by unruly demonstrations and the use of violence both on the floor of the Diet and in the streets?

In practice, when the stakes seemed important enough, they have chosen violence and the nonparliamentary path. In 1954, 1956, 1959–60, and 1965 in particular, they have engaged in systematically planned campaigns involving the use of violence on the floor and in the corridors of the Diet in desperate attempts to prevent the enactment of legislation affecting the powers of the police, the composition of local boards of education, the revision of the security treaty between the United States and Japan, and the enactment of a treaty with South Korea. These are merely the most dramatic instances of minority obstructionism. Despite occasional periods of moderate reconciliation—such as that resulting from Prime Minister Ikeda's "low posture" strategy—the "confrontation," as it is called, of Socialist against Liberal Democratic policies in the Diet has been recurrent and bitter in the extreme. This is one of the most conspicuous and worrisome characteristics of the Japanese Diet. A sizable segment of its members seem not to be really committed to the use of the parliamentary process.

A second characteristic is the rather close relationship that exists between the permanent committees of the Diet—which perform its most important legislative functions—and the Ministries and agencies charged with corresponding interests, for example, the Committee on Agriculture and Forestry and the Ministry of the same name, and the Committee on Commerce and Industry and the Ministry of International Trade and Industry. It is widely claimed that what are often called "clientele relationships" have been established which tend in practice to be controlled by the bureaucrats. This troubles those who believe that the professional bureaucracy in Japan tends to be an antidemocratic force and who conceive of the people's representatives in the Diet as providing an effective means of supervision and control over the Civil Service. This is, however, perhaps but another way of saying that in Japan, as in most modern states, the government is not in fact "parliament centered," regardless of what the Constitution and basic laws may stipulate. The concerns and needs of a political system today have grown too vast, too complex, and too specialized for any body of elected popular representatives to provide effective control over anything but the broadest outlines of policy. We live in the day of the administrative state, and this is as true in Japan as it is in England, Russia, and the United States.

The Cabinet

The Constitution vests executive power in the Cabinet. This is a group of political leaders, including eighteen ministers, a chief cabinet secretary, and a director of the Cabinet Legislation Bureau in 1966. It is headed by the Prime Minister. The Constitution requires that all members of the Cabinet be civilians and that a majority of their number, including the Prime Minister, be members of the Diet. In practice, this has meant that the overwhelming majority of the members of all Cabinets under the 1947 Constitution, invariably including the Prime Minister, have been chosen from the membership of the House of Representatives. A few—seldom more than three or four—might also be drawn from the upper house or from circles outside the Diet. The Prime Minister is selected by a formal resolution of the Diet. On such occasions, it is customary for the several parties represented in the Diet to place the names of their respective leaders in nomination for the post. A majority of those present and voting is required for selection, and thus the post goes to the leader of the majority party or majority coalition in the lower house. The vote in the lower house is controlling and overrides any contrary decision that might be made in the upper house.

Once chosen, the Prime Minister then selects the other members of the Cabinet. Their numbers vary somewhat, and have ranged in recent years from fifteen to twenty. All are technically of equal rank but actually only twelve have "portfolios," that is, they preside over departments called *Ministries*: the Ministers of Justice, Foreign Affairs, Finance, Education, Welfare, Agriculture and Forestry, International Trade and Industry, Transportation, Postal Services, Labor, Construction, and Local Autonomy. The remainder lack "portfolios" and are called *Ministers of State*. Actually, jobs such as the vice-premiership; the chairmanship of the Atomic Energy Commission; the director-generalships of the Administrative Management Agency, the Defense Agency, the Economic Planning Agency, and the Science and Technology Agency; or the chief secretaryship of the Cabinet are often parceled out among them. Although largely free to choose whom he wants to serve in his Cabinet, a Prime Minister is politically obligated to apportion these posts so as to maximize the support behind his own position. A very delicate weighing and balancing operation is involved. Once having selected his colleagues, the Prime Minister is also free to remove them from office at his discretion, provided, of course, that his political position is firm enough to survive the consequences. Strong Prime Ministers like Mr. Yoshida have both appointed and removed large numbers of Ministers.

Since 1947, Prime Ministers have been much more durable than Cabinets (Table 7-1). Mr. Yoshida presided over five different cabinets, for example, from 1946 to 1954, Mr. Hatoyama over three, Mr. Kishi over four, and Mr. Ikeda over seven. The average life of a Cabinet during this period was only nine and a half months, but the average term in office of the Prime Ministers

TABLE 7-1

BRIEF CHRONOLOGY OF POSTWAR JAPANESE CABINETS

Dates	Prime Minister [a]	Reorganizations
Aug. 17, 1945–Oct. 9, 1945	Higashikuni Naruhiko	
Oct. 9, 1945–May 22, 1946	Shidehara Kijuro	
May 22, 1946–May 24, 1947	Yoshida Shigeru	First
May 24, 1947–Mar. 10, 1948	Katayama Tetsu	
Mar. 10, 1948–Oct. 15, 1948	Ashida Hitoshi	
Oct. 15, 1948–Feb. 16, 1949	Yoshida Shigeru	Second
Feb. 16, 1949–Oct. 30, 1952	Yoshida Shigeru	Third
Oct. 30, 1952–May 21, 1953	Yoshida Shigeru	Fourth
May 21, 1953–Dec. 10, 1954	Yoshida Shigeru	Fifth
Dec. 10, 1954–Mar. 19, 1955	Hatoyama Ichiro	First
Mar. 19, 1955–Nov. 22, 1955	Hatoyama Ichiro	Second
Nov. 22, 1955–Dec. 23, 1956	Hatoyama Ichiro	Third
Dec. 23, 1956–Feb. 25, 1957	Ishibashi Tanzan	
Feb. 25, 1957–July 10, 1957	Kishi Nobusuke	First
July 10, 1957–June 12, 1958	Kishi Nobusuke	Second
June 12, 1958–June 18, 1959	Kishi Nobusuke	Third
June 18, 1959–July 19, 1960	Kishi Nobusuke	Fourth
July 19, 1960–Dec. 8, 1960	Ikeda Hayato	First
Dec. 8, 1960–July 18, 1961	Ikeda Hayato	Second
July 18, 1961–July 18, 1962	Ikeda Hayato	Third
July 18, 1962–July 18, 1963	Ikeda Hayato	Fourth
July 18, 1963–Dec. 9, 1963	Ikeda Hayato	Fifth
Dec. 9, 1963–July 18, 1964	Ikeda Hayato	Sixth
July 18, 1964–Nov. 11, 1964	Ikeda Hayato	Seventh
Nov. 11, 1964–June 3, 1965	Sato Eisaku	First
June 3, 1965–July 31, 1966	Sato Eisaku	Second
July 31, 1966–Dec. 3, 1966	Sato Eisaku	Third
Dec. 3, 1966–	Sato Eisaku	Fourth

[a] All Prime Ministers except Katayama Tetsu have represented conservative parties.

from 1945 through June, 1965, was twenty-four months, ranging from Mr. Ishibashi's brief two months to more than seven years for Mr. Yoshida. During this entire period, there has only been one Cabinet headed by a Socialist—the Katayama government, a weak Socialist-conservative coalition that lasted for nine and one-half months in 1947–48. All the rest have been led by conservative politicians.

Cabinets fall, and new Cabinets arise, for complex reasons. Since the conservative dominance has been so complete, parliamentary successes by the opposition party or formal votes of lack of confidence in the lower house have seldom brought down a Cabinet. More often, intraparty and interfactional differences on policy or personnel matters within the conservative camp make some reconstitution of the Cabinet advisable. Public dissatisfaction over government policy or scandals involving high party or governmental officials—cleverly nourished and exploited by the opposition—have also been common causes of the dissolution of Cabinets. And there is constant factional and intraparty pressure on all Cabinets to step aside in favor of other deserving colleagues. This pressure is so strong on any Prime Minister that frequent Cabinet changes are almost the necessary political price for his own continuance in power.

This lack of stability at the Cabinet level does not, however, mean that there is a comparable instability in major national policies. The offices are rotated within the same party or at least within the general conservative camp. The Prime Ministership, and to some extent the Foreign Ministership, does not change with the same frequency. And the administrative vice-ministers, who for the most part actually run the Ministries and agencies, are always career civil servants of long service and experience. These factors make for a considerable amount of policy stability in what otherwise might seem a highly unstable situation.

The Cabinet's functions might be described as both formal and informal. Some of the latter have already been mentioned. Under the guidance of the Prime Minister, for example, it serves as a leadership element for the political party or coalition of parties upon whose support its position depends. Again, Cabinets provide a vehicle for the recognition and reward of loyal or able party service. These are important functions, although less frequently noted than are its formal legal responsibilities. Chief among the latter is its role as the highest executive authority in Japan. It is the Cabinet that is by law responsible for such major executive tasks as preparing and submitting the annual budget—which means, essentially, planning the over-all activities of the state for the coming year—managing the nation's foreign and domestic affairs, administering the Civil Service and controlling the administrative branches of the government, submitting bills to the Diet, executing the laws, and regularly informing the Diet and the people of the state of the nation. It is thus a form of collective chief executive. And, since the Diet is actually incapable of providing policy guidance, its authority also extends to the formulation, or at least advance approval, of practically all major policies of state. Beyond this, it performs a number of other functions. It issues Cabinet orders in pursuance of law, it convokes extraordinary sessions of the Diet, advises the Emperor about the dissolution of the Diet and the proclamation of general elections, and appoints the justices of the Supreme Court. The Cabinet, therefore, possesses practically all the major leadership or executive powers of state at the national level.

Under the present Constitution, Japanese Cabinets exercise their formidable powers through a system of collective responsibility; that is, all members of the Cabinet are jointly responsible for any policy or decision officially taken by the Cabinet. In practice, this means that the Cabinet acts by consensus, or unanimous decision—the traditionally approved way of making group decisions in Japan. Formal votes are rarely, if ever, taken. Issues are discussed until some general agreement is reached and this then becomes the decision of the Cabinet. Any member seriously dissenting from this decision is expected to resign or face dismissal by the Prime Minister.

The Cabinet's relationship with the Diet is, of course, one of the most important aspects of any Cabinet's activities, especially since the Constitution has deliberately made them mutually interdependent. The relations between the House of Representatives and the Cabinet are particularly close. The House of Councillors, since it cannot be dissolved and has but secondary and inferior powers, stands in somewhat different circumstances. The Cabinet is, to begin with, the creature of the Diet—ultimately of the lower house—through the Diet's power to select the Prime Minister. Cabinet members are further made responsible to the Diet through their duty to attend sessions of both houses and their committees and to reply to questions about their policies when officially requested to do so by Diet members. Again, the Diet is legally free to accept, amend, or reject bills submitted by the Cabinet—in practice they accept most of them—or to grant or refuse the funds which are necessary for the implementation of the Cabinet's programs.

Either house of the Diet is also free to level resolutions of impeachment against individual Cabinet members, while the lower house may adopt a resolution of no confidence or reject a resolution of confidence in the Cabinet as a whole, or refuse to support some major piece of legislation sponsored by the Cabinet—which amounts to a vote of lack of confidence. A vote of no confidence or the refusal to pass major Cabinet-backed bills are the most drastic means at the disposal of the lower house for the enforcement of ministerial responsibility to the will of the house. A formal expression of lack of confidence automatically presents the Cabinet with two choices—it must, within a ten-day period, resign en masse or it must dissolve the House of Representatives and call for a general election to select the members of a new House. If it does the latter, the Cabinet must still resign upon the first convocation of the new Diet after the election, leaving the members of this new Diet free to reinstate or replace the former Prime Minister as they see fit. These are all devices for insuring the responsibility of Cabinets to the Diet.

Responsibility runs both ways in this relationship, however. Since the members of the Cabinet are high party officials and dispensers of patronage through both legislative and administrative channels, they have substantial influence over the actions of at least their own majority party or coalition in the Diet. They can usually advance or hamper the political careers of individual members. In practice, too, party discipline is rigorously enforced against their delegations holding seats in the Diet. Serious backbench insurrections against Cabinet leadership—as distinguished from interfactional squabbles—are almost unknown in the Japanese Diet. The ultimate weapon of the Cabinet against a refractory lower house, however, is the power of dissolution, which has the consequence of forcing all members to stand for re-election. Election campaigns are very costly in Japan, and the outcome is by no means always certain. Members of the House of Representatives do not lightly court the expense and uncertainty following upon dissolution and a new general election. To be sure, it is a cost and risk shared by the majority of the Cabinet itself, who are members of the lower house, but their financial connections are apt to be superior and their seats safer than the average. Considerations of this sort tend to make Diet members follow the Cabinet's leadership and loyally support its programs both in committee and on the floor of the House. What problems occur in the ranks of the majority party are almost always the result of factional intrigues and maneuvering.

In executive-legislative relationships, therefore, the Cabinet is the dominant element. This does not imply, however, that the Cabinet by itself provides the ultimate leadership of the Japanese state, for the Cabinet's legal or formal role is qualified in several ways. One of the most important checks against unbridled Cabinet power is the existence of dissident factions within the majority party. To succeed, a Liberal Democratic Cabinet must maintain a delicate balance among what the Japanese call the "mainstream" factions (composed of party members who support the Prime Minister). In setting policy or making decisions, the Cabinet must always take into account the interests of these groups as well as those of the "antimainstream" factions (composed of members who, although belonging to the Liberal Democratic Party's delegation in the Diet, are opposed to its present leadership and are promoting their own candidate for the Prime Ministership). The Cabinet is thus subject to continuous influence and partial controls from elements within its own party. For quite different reasons, the Cabinet is also constantly influenced by the "advice" of the professional bureaucracy. At the operating level the major ministries of state are headed by career civil servants with the title of administrative vice-minister. This group meets regularly and frequently with the Director of the Cabinet Secretariat and the Director of the Cabinet Bureau of Legislation as a sort of "little cabinet"—and it is far better informed about most matters of policy and administration than are the members of the Cabinet.

As technicians operating in highly technical fields, these bureaucrats decide a great many matters, which are then sent up for fairly routine approval by the Cabinet proper. In this manner, the professional bureaucracy, through its own leaders, exercises a very considerable influence on many Cabinet actions. To some extent, this influence is counterbalanced by the extensive professional and technical staff that is attached directly to the Prime Minister. Known as the Office of the Prime Minister, this staff contained more than 29,000 employees in 1965, exclusive of the National Defense Agency. It serves as a professional staff for the Cabinet and somewhat reduces the Cabinet's dependence on the bureaucracy in the regular Ministries and agencies. In sum, primary political power in contemporary Japan rests with the Cabinet, and in particular with the Prime Minister; they probably perform more decision making of major importance than any other formal unit of government. But, as we have seen, they are subject to constant interaction with and substantial influence from several other official and unofficial groups. There is no simple answer to this question of political primacy.

The Bureaucracy

Ever since the Meiji Restoration of 1867–68—which might itself be described as a sort of bureaucratic *coup d'état*—the importance of the bureaucracy has bulked very large in the Japanese political system. The founders of modern Japan were not themselves democrats and they were not particularly concerned to establish a "civil service" in our sense of the term, that is, a politically neutral, professionalized service dedicated to the achievement of democratically set goals by means determined and supervised by the representatives of the people. The conception of a bureaucrat as a "public servant" was almost totally absent from both Japanese political theory and practice until it was inserted in Article 15 of the new Constitution by Americans in 1946. Before 1946, a Japanese bureaucrat was officially viewed as a chosen servant of the Emperor, a politically and socially superior being who derived status and privileges from his Imperial connection. The old Tokugawa adage, *kanson mimpi* ("officials honored, the people despised"), well describes the prewar bureaucrat's attitude toward the public. A tradition of this depth and intensity dies hard. Despite a number of postwar reform attempts, there is a good deal yet to be done before the average bureaucrat successfully negotiates the transition to the status of "public servant."

As in many other countries, postwar times brought to Japan an enormous inflation in the size of her bureaucracy. Just before the war in 1940, for example, if we exclude the military and certain temporary employees, the Japanese national government had 231,898 employees. In 1965 the comparable figure was 1,632,241, a slightly more than sevenfold increase (Table 7-2). In 1963, the bureaucracy in Japan—including the civilian employees of both national and local governments and the military—totaled about 4,000,000 persons; thus roughly one out of every twelve members of the labor force worked for the government. This is a very sizable number, but for our purposes it is the higher civil service which is most important. These higher civil servants may be loosely defined as those individuals who attain the first, second, or third grades in the administrative service. In 1965, there were only 8,391 such positions in the entire national government, of which perhaps half were really important. Access to these positions is usually restricted to persons who pass the higher Civil Service examinations. The higher bureaucracy is thus not a very large group; it probably numbers about four or five thousand people, and replenishes itself at a rate of two to three hundred members at the bottom per year. Its training and preparation are rigorous.

Government service has always been and still is today regarded as one of the most desirable careers open to young Japanese. Access to its higher levels is achieved through an outstanding academic record. Influential connections also help. In elementary school, the brighter students are constantly faced with the necessity of getting the highest possible grades in an endless series of difficult examinations. Brilliant performances in these provide entrance to the best high schools and ultimately to the best universities. The equivalent of an honors degree from a good university is particularly essential to anyone hoping to take and pass the higher Civil Service examinations. A few universities in prewar times acquired a practical monopoly over access to these higher positions. The elite of the prewar administrative service, for example, consisted of those who took and passed the higher Civil Service examination while still students, then graduated from Imperial universities, and went on to achieve the first or second grades of the Civil Service. Among these, ninety-two per cent were graduates of Tokyo Imperial University's Law Department and four per cent of Kyoto Imperial's Law Department.

The tests were largely set and graded by members of the law faculties of these schools, and their graduates, once in the higher services, were given preferential status and advancement by their fellow alumni of earlier classes and higher rank. This situation has improved since the war. One now encounters many more graduates of Kyoto, Waseda, Keio, Hitotsubashi, Nihon, and other colleges, but a pronounced "old-school tie" prejudice, still fostered by a Tokyo University clique, is readily discernible. In the 1949–59 period, for example, sixty-nine per cent of all Japanese higher civil servants were graduates of Tokyo University, and at the level of vice-ministers and bureau chiefs the proportion exceeded eighty per cent. It should also be noted that the courses of study and tests leading to a Civil Service career have been somewhat broadened in comparison with their excessively narrow and legalistic

TABLE 7-2

JAPANESE GOVERNMENT EMPLOYEES [a]

A. NATIONAL GOVERNMENT EMPLOYEES

Fiscal Year	Total	Total	General account (except National Defense Agency)	Special accounts	Government corporations
	Total	National Defense Agency			
1949	1,567,638	......	424,408	495,503	647,727
1950	1,578,585	75,100	431,813	498,922	572,750
1951	1,488,401	75,100	428,000	493,124	492,177
1952	1,507,345	118,953	413,678	335,505	639,209
1953	1,528,442	123,153	416,849	339,918	648,522
1954	1,503,334	164,540	347,083	334,139	657,572
1955	1,353,810	195,811	340,709	335,031	664,259
1956	1,565,248	215,004	340,657	338,938	670,649
1957	1,580,264	223,502	341,213	341,042	674,507
1958	1,627,240	242,718	352,279	353,955	678,288
1959	1,665,868	254,800	362,087	366,932	682,049
1960	1,696,320	263,205	361,260	383,369	688,486
1961	1,767,393	268,334	373,774	428,651	696,634
1962	1,825,666	273,779	385,732	454,737	711,418
1963	1,851,800	275,534	390,746	462,370	723,150
1964	1,878,193	276,581	306,971	559,393	735,248
1965	1,910,305	278,064	308,016	570,728	735,497

B. LOCAL GOVERNMENTAL EMPLOYEES (1963)

Classification	Total	Prefectures	Six large cities	Other cities	Towns and villages
Total	2,110,348	1,300,066	131,239	404,540	244,264
Regular personnel	1,247,796	461,226	124,950	394,061	240,693
General	625,736	258,999	33,766	179,490	145,823
Tax	84,411	26,461	5,770	29,056	22,650
Maritime	2,262	1,778	100	158	187
Research	11,658	11,037	475	131	15
Medical	77,064	31,066	5,607	22,842	13,548
Fire defense	42,785	9,783	8,373	22,426	1,826
Enterprises	136,576	38,884	43,999	47,842	2,752
Technical workers	264,304	83,218	26,860	92,116	53,892
Educational personnel	724,764	704,052	6,289	10,479	3,571
Police	137,788	137,788	......	......	......

[a] *Nihon Tōkei Nenkan*, 1965.

prewar counterparts. A heavy emphasis is still placed, however, on the applicant's ability to recall legal and technical details.

A college graduate who has passed the higher Civil Service examinations normally enters the service as a sixth-grade employee. If possible, he will choose one of the more important Ministries that has promotional paths leading to the heart of political and administrative power in the Japanese system, and which may lead, after retirement, to a lucrative post in private business or perhaps to an elective political career. Since retirement comes early in most Ministries—at forty-nine or fifty on the average—and pensions are markedly inadequate, such post-retirement considerations are important. The most promising careers before the war lay in the Ministry of Internal Affairs. Today, they are to be found primarily in the Ministry of Finance, and secondarily in the Ministries of International Trade and Industry or Agriculture and Forestry. To some, the Foreign Ministry is also attractive as a sort of special case.

Once having been accepted by a particular Ministry, the new civil servant's career is apt to lie primarily within that Ministry. A recent survey of inter-ministry mobility demonstrates that in the 1949–59 period a third of the major civil servants had served in only a single ministry, another third had served in more than one ministry but had returned ultimately to their ministry of first assignment, while only the remaining third had been permanently transferred to other ministries or agencies. Interministry rivalry and suspicion are acute, and administrative cooperation across ministerial boundaries is difficult to achieve. Displays of individual initiative or brilliance on the part of junior employees are not highly valued. Loyalty and obedience to superiors, tact, anonymity, patience, and a capacity for the endless details and rituals of administration are the normal virtues. Personal and job security is complete; accountability to the public is practically nil. Yet, since the initial recruiting process is so rigorous and highly selective, intelligent and able men are obtained. And they normally move up with some rapidity toward the pinnacle of bureaucratic achievement, a vice-ministership.

The higher bureaucracy in Japan is deeply involved in politics for several reasons. First, such involvement is a solidly entrenched part of the Japanese tradition. Politics, even of the party variety, has been a prominent and constant concern of the higher administrators ever since the Restoration. Second, the fact that the national legislature is weak and ill-equipped to deal with the complex problems of a modern society has left a vacuum which bureaucratic expertise and enterprise have gladly filled. Third, in modern times, political decisions have become so inextricably mingled with problems of administration and technology that it is unrealistic to think of bureaucracy and politics as separate categories. The bureaucrats and specialists of Japan, for example, have a great deal to say about the incidence of taxation, the granting of licenses and permits, the determination of bank rates, the availability and allocation of credit and public subsidies, and the location and construction of public works. All of these are decisions which vitally affect the interests of important and organized sectors of the Japanese population—business, finance, labor, agriculture, and so forth. It is scarcely remarkable that these interests seek to influence critically placed bureaucrats, or that they try to reinforce this influence by promises of sinecure jobs upon retirement, gifts of stock, lavish entertainment, or outright bribes. A good deal of corruption, on both major and minor scales, is present in such relationships. Proof lies in the annual reports of the Board of Audit, which showed in fiscal 1964 alone 644 cases of misappropriation of public funds totaling some 2,790,000,000 yen ($7,750,-000). The bureaucrats become involved in politics in this fashion, too.

But since the war, a fourth type of bureaucratic involvement in politics has become particularly notable. Upon retirement, substantial numbers of the higher bureaucracy have in recent years run for elective political office. In 1963, for example, at least seventy-six members of the lower house (sixteen per cent of the total membership) and fifty-five members of the upper house (twenty-two per cent) were former career bureaucrats. In almost all cases, they were members of the Liberal Democratic Party. Again, some thirty-five per cent of the membership of the Cabinets holding office between 1954 and 1961 were former bureaucrats. These men have gained formal political status and power partially as a result of their own knowledge and ability. But they have often been greatly aided in doing so by the financial support of contacts made during their years of public service and the electoral support of groups associated with the work of their former Ministry. In this manner, large numbers of former bureaucrats—not noted as a group for their dedication to democratic causes—have gained Cabinet or parliamentary office. Once in office, their professional knowledge of particular aspects of government and their close connections with the bureaucracy have given them unusual prominence and influence. This might in some cases make for greater efficiency, but there is considerable concern in Japan about its effect on the democratic content and practice of government.

Local Government

Prior to the effectuation of the new Constitution in 1947, Japan had an extremely centralized form of government, in two different senses. First, all political power was legally and theoretically concentrated in the person of the Emperor. Second, all political power was legally and actually concentrated at the national level; local governments enjoyed no autonomous rights. They were created and controlled by the national government in Tokyo. The American authorities who controlled the Allied Occupation of Japan objected strenuously to the continuance of this system. Their political goal was the democratization of Japan, and they seem to have felt that democratic institutions and practices flourish in direct proportion to their closeness to the people. In other words, the Japanese system of government required drastic decentralization through the granting of extensive rights of local self-government to the prefectures, cities, towns, and villages of Japan. In this way, they could be made directly responsive to local desires and conditions and their democratic potential greatly enhanced.

Relatively little thought appears to have been given to any deleterious effects which such a decentralization of authority might have on the strength or efficiency of the national government. In fact, such a consequence was probably regarded as desirable. The result of such views on the part of the Occupation authorities was, first, the enshrinement of the principle of local autonomy in Article 92 of the new Constitution and, second, the enactment of the Local Autonomy Law on April 17, 1947. The combination of these with other related legislation provides the legal basis for the present system of local government in Japan. Judged by earlier Japanese standards, this is a highly decentralized system, although it is, of course, not as decentralized as the federally organized system that exists in the United States. Japan technically still has a unified system of government.

At its highest level below the nation, local government in Japan is organized into forty-six prefectures (Fig. 7-2). The prefectures are governed, subject to national laws, by a popularly elected governor and a single-house legislature. The total territory of each prefecture is then further subdivided into cities, towns, and villages. These are the lowest units of self-government in Japan— with the exception of Tokyo's self-governing districts, which comprise a special case. There is nothing corresponding to our unincorporated territories in Japan. Each city, town, or village directly elects its own mayor and single-house assembly. All these local governments, from the prefecture down, are semiparliamentary systems, in which the chief executives and their assemblies are rendered mutually interdependent through their respective powers of dissolution and votes of nonconfidence. The law also extends very considerable powers of local self-government to all these levels and units and, thereby, denies the exercise of such powers to agencies of the national government.

This is a brief description of the legal position of local governmental units in Japan. Their actual position deviates from this in several important respects. They are not really autonomous to anything like the degree anticipated by the law. In practice, local officials spend most of their time administering the policies and business of the national Ministries at the local level. The laws and ordinances which they adopt are quite apt to be carbon copies of model statutes developed initially in Tokyo. Furthermore, few, if any, local governments are financially self-supporting. Twenty per cent or more of their essential revenues are normally derived from subsidies and grants-in-aid received largely from the national government. This pronounced degree of fiscal dependency plus the long-ingrained bureaucratic habit of looking to Tokyo and the national government for guidance detracts greatly from the actual degree of autonomy enjoyed by the prefectures, cities, towns, and villages of Japan.

The Judicial System

The judicial system, like so many of the other institutions of prewar Japan, was greatly changed by the Occupation. Anglo-American common law principles were widely introduced into a system which had been largely European in derivation. The legal, civil, and political rights of Japanese citizens were greatly expanded; the government and its servants were made far more accountable for their actions; and, in general, a serious attempt was made to introduce into Japanese society the almost completely foreign principle of the rule of law. A series of basic reforms in the judicial system lay at the root of these attempts.

In prewar Japan, the courts had been, in effect, an arm of the national government, administered by the Ministry of Justice. Under the Constitution of 1947, this was completely changed. Article 76 vests "the whole judicial power" in a Supreme Court and in such inferior courts as may be established by law. This provision creates a judicial branch of the government with an independent status that is substantially equal to that enjoyed by the legislative or executive branches. The Supreme Court is given complete administrative control over all inferior courts, and is further explicitly given the right of judicial review, that is, the power to determine the constitutionality of any law, order, regulation, or official act. The fifteen judges of the Supreme Court are appointed by the Cabinet, except for the Chief Judge who is appointed by the Emperor upon nomination by the Cabinet. The judges serve for life, subject to decennial referenda by the voters upon their records. Beneath the Supreme Court in 1965 was a hierarchy of inferior courts ranging from eight High Courts through forty-nine District Courts (with attached Family Courts) to 560 Summary Courts at the base of the pyramid. Together with a large number of civil and family conciliation commissions, each composed of one judge and two intelligent and experienced laymen and intended to provide facilities for the out-of-court settlement of disputes, these are the principal components of the present Japanese judicial system.

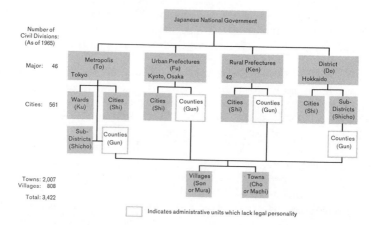

FIGURE 7-2. THE STRUCTURE OF JAPANESE LOCAL GOVERNMENT.

The courts, although in a technical sense they seem to be functioning reasonably well, do not play as important a role as might be expected. The Japanese are a rather remarkably nonlitigious people. They are traditionally suspicious of the courts and of formal legal processes, and have a pronounced preference for settling disputes by informal methods of conciliation and mediation. These methods are highly developed, especially in the countryside, and normally recourse will be had to the courts only when the issue is very serious and these older folkish techniques of mediated settlement have failed.

From a political standpoint, few judicial issues have aroused more comment and controversy than the Supreme Court's American-inspired power of judicial review. This is completely foreign to the Japanese legal tradition and many have watched with interest to see whether or not the Supreme Court would actually make use of this power and occasionally declare an act of the Diet, of a Ministry, or of a local government unconstitutional, thus asserting its right to play a positive role in national politics in the way that the United States Supreme Court does. Since 1947 there have only been two or three cases

—none of particular importance—in which the Supreme Court has held laws enacted since the end of the Occupation to be unconstitutional.

In the light of such a record, it would seem highly improbable, under present circumstances at least, that the Supreme Court will ever make significant use of the power of judicial review.

Chapter *8*

GOVERNMENTAL
PERFORMANCE

Thus far we have been discussing what might be termed the "input" phase of Japan's governmental operations—the environmental and historical factors which condition the functioning of the government, the process by which those who influence or control its operations are selected, and the nature of the machinery by which decisions are made and administered. Yet, as with any productive process, one must ultimately be concerned with its product, with the "output" as well as the "input" phase of its operations. How effectively do the "products" of government meet the needs of the society's time and circumstances? How well do they satisfy the various demands that government must consider in its decisions? How do they affect the equilibrium of the political process itself? These are the tests by which a political system is ultimately judged both by its own members and by foreign observers. Let us then look briefly at this part of Japan's record.

In examining the output aspects of Japan's political system, what standards of evaluation should we apply? No very precise measure of accomplishment has been devised, and, consequently, we usually render our comparative political judgments in terms that are more resonant than they are accurate or informative. The problem is difficult, and we have no promising new formula to submit. But one thing we should definitely guard against is the facile tendency of many Westerners, and Japanese as well, to judge Japan's political performance against British or American standards of accomplishment—and even these are not realistically stated but set forth in the idealized terms of the democratic theorist. Japan's modern political heritage and circumstances bear very faint resemblance to those of Great Britain or the United States. They are far closer to those of Italy or some of the more recently developing states of Eastern Europe.

If a society's cultural background, political history, and political forces are this different from those of the major democratic states of the West, we should not expect its political views and behavior to parallel those of these states. Yet this is precisely the assumption that is too often made by both foreigners and Japanese sitting in judgment on Japan's recent political record. Japan has an Asian culture and a primarily Asian heritage. Its significant political associations with the West date back only about a hundred years. It is too much to hope that a hundred years of largely adverse political experience will soon, if ever, produce in Japan the same type of democratic system that has been four hundred years or more in the making in Great Britain and the United States. It is far more fruitful and constructive to look on the Japanese political record as an example of what can happen to Asian and other underdeveloped societies and polities.

In describing the performance of a foreign political system, we who have always lived in a politically democratic society tend to concentrate on the degree to which the foreign system achieves certain fundamental values embodied in basic democratic theory. The phrase "popular and responsible government" sums up many of these values. In Japan's case, great pains have been taken to establish optimal conditions for the development of such a "popular and responsible government." To what extent has this been accomplished? Inevitably, the answer is complicated, and we perhaps had better examine first the "popular" element in the phrase and then the "responsible" element.

Few modern states can equal the scope of opportunities legally available to the Japanese people to vote for both national and local governments. The major political offices at all levels are elective, elections are held regularly, and the right to participate is as free and untrammeled by sex, age, residential, or other restrictions as one will find anywhere. Beyond this, a number of special methods of popular participation are provided for: popular plebiscites on constitutional amendments, regular referendums on Supreme Court judges, and rights of initiative and recall at the local level. Also, such informal types of political organizations as interest groups are rapidly increasing in numbers and importance and are assuming many of the forms familiar to us in the West.

The Japanese citizen has, therefore, numerous opportunities to participate in his political system, and he ordinarily makes good use of them. The Japanese voting rates, for example, are extraordinarily high, judged by either Asian or Western standards. But many Japanese and foreign observers ask: How well informed and how democratically meaningful is this high level of political participation? The answer has been disappointing. Factual studies indicate that in Japan—as in the United States, too, one should not forget—a great many voters and members of interest groups are primarily influenced by traditional loyalties, boss rule, communal solidarity, and other factors generally regarded as antipathetic to a democratic system. Japanese politics is thus a fascinating mixture of traditional, modern, democratic, and undemocratic elements. This mixture is to be found, incidentally, both in the conservative and in the more modern-appearing socialist camps, and it warns us against accepting this high rate of popular political participation as a sign of meaningful democratic performance.

When we come to evaluate the "responsibility" of Japanese governmental performance, we find that all the normal structural and procedural safeguards to insure that government is really responsible to the people have been elaborately built into the Japanese political system at all levels. These safeguards include elections, recall, referendums, initiative, votes of no confidence, rights of interpellation, governmental fiscal accountability, and so forth. Their introduction into what had been a distinctly oligarchical political system has appreciably increased the responsibility and accountability of Japan's elected political leaders to the public. Elected officials have become far more powerful in Japanese politics than they were before the war, and the importance of elections has risen correspondingly. To become Prime Minister or the governor of a prefecture or mayor of a town, a Japanese politician must usually run the gantlet of several successful election campaigns, and he obviously cannot flout or ignore public opinion as the prewar leadership did. This increased need to win elections and to court public favor does not tell the whole story, however. In practice, the elected leaders share political power with both the bureaucracy and the representatives of a variety of influential private interests. These two groups are not effectively responsible to public control in Japan, although to be fair, there are few political systems in which they are. In Japan, however, the relative weakness of the "public service" concept, the traditional ascendancy of group over popular interests, and the arbitrary spirit of the bureaucracy magnify these shortcomings in the degree of the government's responsibility to the people.

Since World War II, the Japanese government has displayed distinctly more interest in the economic than in the political aspects of its performance. There can be no doubt that its highest priority has been the economic rehabilitation and development of Japan. The reasons are self-evident. Postwar Japanese governments inherited a country devastated by bombing and blockade, an economy in shambles, a people in desperate need of food and jobs, and a world economic position and prospect that looked dire indeed. The enormity of the challenge was obvious. Successive governments, at first with Occupation prodding and assistance and, since roughly 1950, on their own initiative, have concentrated on improving the country's economic circumstances, and it is in this area that they have achieved their most spectacular successes.

One has only to look back to the situation in Japan at the end of the war to comprehend how dazzling the improvement in her economic conditions has been. In August, 1945, at least a quarter of the national wealth and a third of the nation's industrial machinery and equipment had been destroyed; production figures stood at about one-tenth the 1935–36 average. Inflation was rampant, and within a year prices for food and clothing on the free market rose from seventy to one hundred and forty times the prewar averages. Expenditures for food comprised about eighty per cent of the total family budget, and the average city worker got only about 1,600 calories of food a day instead of the 2,150 calories required to keep him strong and healthy. People were still living in air raid shelters, and necessities of every sort were in acutely short supply. The gross national product in 1947 was about $3.6 billion.

In 1965, twenty years after the end of the war, all major indexes of national and per capita prosperity had not only regained their prewar averages but, in all cases, had greatly exceeded them. Japan's gross national product in 1965 was about $78.4 billion. This represented a 13.4 per cent increase over the previous year in nominal terms, and a 7.8 per cent increase in real terms. Her annual rate of real economic growth, which had averaged 4.6 per cent for the years 1926–39, averaged 9.4 per cent for the twelve years from 1954 to 1965 and reached 15 per cent in 1959, one of the highest figures in the world. Japan's economic recovery since the war is rivaled only by that of West Germany, and her growth rate is superior to the rate claimed by such forced-draft and totalitarian economies as that of the Chinese People's Republic. This vast improvement in economic conditions is not only a statistic; it is reflected in the people's standard of living, which on a per capita basis is now about double that of the best prewar years. Although it is still substantially below that of the United States and Great Britain, it is very high by Asian standards. What were once luxury items, quite unthinkable for the average budget, are now becoming commonplace—television sets, refrigerators, electric washing machines, high-quality foods, sizable quantities of meat and dairy products, and even automobiles. The very body measurements of the Japanese have changed in response to an enriched diet and better living conditions; the average child is taller and more robust than were his parents and his life expectancy is greater.

All these changes constitute basic improvements in the way of life of the average Japanese family. But they are not without their darker side. The incidence of economic prosperity has been uneven. Much of the labor force employed by medium- and small-sized industries remains today in relatively depressed circumstances, as do many of that too-often overlooked category of laborers known as "temporary employees." In recent years, the increase of prosperity in the countryside has lagged appreciably behind that in the cities. Another negative factor has been the government's failure to regulate or police important aspects of the economy effectively. The interests of the consumer and of the public are not infrequently slighted on behalf of some better-organized and more influential group, especially big business. A Fair Trade Commission has been established to police and regulate monopolistic practices, price fixing, advertising, and so forth, but its powers are not extensive and its accomplishments to date, although helpful, leave much to be desired. A good deal remains to be done to distribute the benefits of Japan's present prosperity more equitably, but this should not be permitted to obscure the really remarkable improvements that have occurred in the basic economic circumstances of the Japanese people. It would be overly facile to assign the total credit for these to the Japanese government, but it would be equally wrong to deny that effective political leadership has contributed heavily to the successes achieved.

Since the war, the government has also recognized an entirely new range of obligations in the field of social security. Before the war, the government took on very limited obligations in this area. It was primarily the duty of the family to support any of its members who became incapacitated because of injury, illness, old age, or adverse economic circumstances. In fact, much of the strength of the traditional family system derived from its role as a welfare agency. The new Constitution changed this situation. Article 25 states that "all people shall have the right to maintain the minimum standards of wholesome and cultured living" and that "in all spheres of life, the State shall use its endeavors for the promotion and extension of social welfare and security, and of public health." These are, of course, vague statements, but they have served to make welfare and social security explicit responsibilities of the state.

The Japanese government has established a complex network of assistance programs which includes unemployment, health, old-age, survivors', seamen's and industrial accident insurance plans. These are supplemented by government-supported vocational guidance and training centers, employment exchanges, a child-welfare program, and aid for the physically handicapped. The sum of all these services scarcely amounts to a cradle-to-grave security program. Many of the programs, for example, are applicable only to the regular employees of establishments employing five or more workers, thus excluding the large portion of the labor force who happen to be engaged in agriculture, forestry, fisheries, and service or family industries. Also, the financial benefits involved remain markedly inadequate to the needs of those concerned. Still, by 1964, over forty million persons were receiving some form of family or individual assistance under the Daily Life Protection Law, and nearly forty-four million were covered by National Health Insurance. In 1965 the government was devoting about fourteen per cent of its annual budget to the support of social security and related matters. This represents rather commendable progress in a brief space of time, and a tremendous change over prewar attitudes and practices.

Another basic concern of the postwar government has been public education. Here again, partially at the behest of the Occupation authorities, the changes since the war have been startling. The elementary and compulsory levels of education were well developed before the war, and the changes that have taken place have been largely designed to liberalize and democratize the system. At the higher levels, however, there have been great expansions of enrollment and changes in structure. In 1940, under the old system, there was a total of forty-seven universities with 81,999 students; by 1964 there were 852,572 students attending 291 colleges and universities. Because of structural changes in the system, these two sets of figures are not totally comparable, but they do give some indication of the expansion in the opportunities for higher education which have taken place in Japan. A higher proportion of the population attends college in Japan today than in almost any other country except the United States. Still, numerous problems remain. Critics of the regime complain bitterly that the government is trying to recentralize control of the educational system under the national Ministry of Education, that it is also trying to indoctrinate Japanese youth with traditional morality and nationalist sentiments through the reintroduction of so-called "morals courses," and that it is systematically repressing freedom of speech and of political opinion on the part of both teachers and students. The entire issue of politics in education is highly controversial and partisan, but, again, it should not be permitted to obscure the great advances which have taken place in this area.

Foreign relations constitute another major field of concern of the government. Actually, however, the Japanese did not take over formal responsibility for their own foreign policy until the end of the Occupation in April, 1952. Since then a succession of Liberal Democratic governments has tended to follow a policy of maintaining close relations with the United States and its Western allies, supplemented by a strong emphasis on the United Nations as a means of settling or ameliorating international disputes. Normally, the government has placed primary emphasis on economic development and the foreign trade upon which Japan's prosperity depends. Postwar governments have also been reluctant to build up Japan's military strength beyond a minimal level, or to push very strongly for the return of the small portion of Japan's lost prewar territories which were considered to be domestic rather than imperial, that is, Okinawa and the Bonins from the United States, and the Kuriles and Southern Sakhalin from the U.S.S.R. The success enjoyed by these foreign policies has been variable. In the vital economic sphere, especially in the field of foreign trade, Japan has done very well. She is able to obtain the raw materials she needs from overseas and to sell more than enough abroad to pay for them. Her problems in this area are never-ending though not critical, however, and range from tariff and other discriminations against Japanese goods in foreign markets to the new forms of trade competition presented or threatened by the modernizing economies of her Asian neighbors, and by trading blocs such as the European Economic Community.

It is far more difficult to determine her degree of success in the foreign-policy field. So much depends on future and unforeseeable developments. Yet, with American aid, Japan has been able to liquidate most of the political costs of defeat. The Treaty of San Francisco restored her to a condition of peace and equality with the majority of her former enemies. A diplomatic agreement with Russia in 1956, while less than a formal treaty of peace, renewed official relationships between the two countries. The negotiation of reparations agreements with her former enemies in Southeast Asia has restored essential relations in this area. Only the Chinese People's Republic, North Korea, and North Vietnam continue to present serious problems in this respect. Beyond this, Japan has gained admission to the United Nations and participates in a normal number of international conferences and actions as a fully sovereign nation.

These are not negligible accomplishments for a country which was defeated in 1945 and occupied as recently as 1952. Still, Japan has regained none of her lost territories, and her government's basic policies on armaments and her pro-American and pro-Western alignment in the cold war have precipitated some of the most spectacular and deep-seated domestic controversies in her postwar history. It is difficult, therefore, to say how effective Japan's governmental performance has been in the foreign-policy area. Perhaps we should limit the verdict and only say that it has so far met and coped satisfactorily with its major and most pressing problems, albeit not to the satisfaction of a sizable segment of the Japanese population.

It would seem from the foregoing account that the over-all output or performance of postwar Japanese governments has been reasonably good. But one would never reach this conclusion from reading the Japanese daily or periodical press or from talking with the majority of her intellectuals. The predominant impression to be gained from such sources is that practically all conservative governments are compounded from a recipe in which the principal ingredients are scurrility, rapacity, reaction, corruption, and inefficiency, and the record of the conservatives is condemned as reflecting such qualities.

To a certain extent, this criticism is rooted in the normal irresponsibility of a partisan group not themselves in power. The political press in Japan has frequently been strongly antigovernment in tone and often sympathetic to socialists and socialist causes. And many people actually believe all that is said about conservative politicians, professional bureaucrats, and big businessmen—the unholy trinity that many think really operates the government almost exclusively for its own benefit.

Behind this belief lies a certain amount of solid evidence. Japanese politics obviously suffers from considerable corruption, graft, and favoritism, and many conservative leaders do feel that Japan, under American influence, has swung too far away from her own past and native course of development. Since these conservative leaders would like to restore some of the older ways and institutions, many Japanese fear that today's conservatives are not significantly different in ideology or action from Japan's prewar leaders. Opposition political leaders are frustrated because they feel they have been denied a proper role in the shaping of national political decisions.

The most important source of opposition, however, lies in the fact that there is a fundamental disagreement between conservatives and progressives over the proper goals, structure, and activities of the state. Japan's intellectuals are largely philosophical Marxists—among the most doctrinaire in the world—and thus tend to be ideological socialists in their politics. The conservative politicians, bureaucrats, and businessmen who control the Japanese government represent very different political views. Between the two lies a yawning chasm. While recognizing the shortcomings of the conservative governments and the justice of some of the charges against them, we should not overlook these governments' amazing records of solid accomplishment in many areas of basic concern to the Japanese people as a whole. There have been a number of fundamental, almost revolutionary, political changes in Japan since the war. They may have been largely initiated by the American Occupation, but they have been carried on by the Japanese people and their government.

Chapter *9*

PROBLEMS AND
PROSPECTS

It would be misleading to discuss Japan's political problems without first emphasizing the level of accomplishment the country has already achieved. Japan is a modern state, and this fact sets her apart from all other Asian countries. Her people are literate and prosperous; her economy is specialized, complex, and advanced; her administration is skilled and professional; her citizenry is politically informed and, increasingly, politically involved as well; and her government is popularly elected and relatively responsive to majority demands. These are not commonplace attributes in contemporary Asia or elsewhere. They both mark the level of Japan's accomplishments and set the context of her present political problems.

Japan's two primary political problems concern the stability and the form of her political system. How stable is it? And, since some change is inevitable, will this be along democratic or authoritarian lines? Although we cannot give a precise answer to such complex questions, we can identify some of the factors that will undoubtedly determine the ultimate answer in the future.

One problem that urgently calls for a remedy is the rigid polarization of the political system between conservative and progressive extremes. The leaders of Japan's conservative forces are mostly elderly men of long experience and considerable ability. They strongly support a mixed economy of private enterprise with very substantial governmental participation. They are closely identified with business and with the professional bureaucracy, and although they accept many of the democratic reforms introduced into postwar Japan, they also favor revising the Constitution and increasing national and governmental authority at the expense of local and popular rights. They distrust and strongly oppose Marxism and Marxists. Yet the leaders of the "progressives," the political opposition in Japan, are almost all Marxists of some sort. These progressive leaders tend to perceive both society and politics in rather narrow and fixed theoretical terms, and this doctrinaire view has not yet been altered by the sobering effects of responsibility in office. They consider the conservatives not only political but also ideological and class enemies. The result is what the left wing likes to describe as a "confrontation between the forces of reaction and the forces of progress."

In such a situation, there is distressingly little room for maneuver or compromise. On issues of major importance, both sides usually take a fairly inflexible stand, and thus impede the functioning of the parliamentary process. The conservatives, with a three-fifths majority in the National Diet, are legally in a position to enact what policies or laws they please. The Socialist Party, therefore, is faced with deciding whether or not to abide by the results of normal parliamentary procedure. In a disturbing number of cases, they have decided not to do so, and have obstructed the parliamentary process by abstaining en masse, by seizing control of the rostrum by force, by immuring the Speaker in his chambers so that he is unable to open or to close a session, and by physically attacking members of the opposition. These tactics on the floor of the Diet are occasionally supplemented by mass demonstrations in the streets, which sometimes erupt into violence, all designed to put additional pressure on the conservative majority.

These systematically planned activities by the major opposition party pose questions about the very foundations of the present Japanese political system. How is public policy to be decided, if not by the normal functioning of a duly established parliament? What is the appropriate political role for a minority party that seems unable to achieve power by legal means in the foreseeable future? What are the merits of the Socialists' charge that they are subjected to a "tyranny of the majority"? On specific issues, it is possible to sympathize with the Socialists, but on the principles involved, it is hard to approve their stand. All parties must abide by the country's Constitution and basic laws if a democratic political system is to be maintained. The Socialists in Japan have refused to follow parliamentary procedures on certain vital issues of foreign and domestic policy. And on such questions as the powers of the police, the abolition of locally elected boards of education, the renewal of the security treaty with the United States, and the revision of the present Japanese Constitution, they have either resorted to illegal means to forestall action by the conservative majority or threatened to do so. So far, these tactics have produced spectacular and worrisome results but not catastrophic ones. Usually, they have neither prevented the conservative majority from taking its desired action nor seriously disrupted the operations of government. But in a situation in which the majority and minority parties so notably lack common ground, serious questions are raised about the future of democracy and the stability of the political system.

Under present circumstances, the danger is perhaps not great. The conservatives are strong enough at the polls, in the Diet, and in their relations with the bureaucracy to overcome the tactics of the opposition with but temporary inconvenience and embarrassment. Up till now, the Socialist Party has confined its obstructionism to particular issues and relatively brief spans of time.

But what would happen if Socialist electoral and parliamentary strength were to increase to approximately that of the conservatives? Although improbable at present, this could happen. Underlying the conservative political dominance in Japan is the unprecedented and broadly shared prosperity of recent years. The conservatives assert that this is their accomplishment and undoubtedly reap great political benefits from this claim. Yet the Japanese economy is by no means immune to recessions, especially since it is heavily dependent on foreign trade and other factors beyond Japan's control. A serious and sustained depression, perhaps originating abroad, could greatly increase Socialist political strength and could even bring a Socialist government to power. The lack of political consensus between the two major parties could then become a far more serious issue than it is today, and the democratic process might suffer accordingly.

Another potential source of trouble is the weakness of the myths and beliefs which underlie Japan's unity and solidarity. Before World War II, the common, even fervent acceptance of the Imperial system provided effective support for Japan's nationhood. But defeat and occupation weakened this sense of unity. These are times of skepticism and spiritual drift in Japan. Many, particularly among the younger generations, are disenchanted with the Imperial myth, and prefer a more rational political symbolism. But the new constitutional system and the spirit of democracy have not yet become firmly enough established in the minds and hearts of the people to provide a satisfactory substitute. Given time and favorable circumstances, perhaps they will, but until then, Japan's adherence to democratic values and processes will remain untested and uncertain. Such eventualities aside, however, the most notable facts about the current Japanese political system undoubtedly are its high degree of modernization, its stability, and the astonishing increase in its democratic content that has taken place since 1945.

BIBLIOGRAPHY

Allen, G. C., *Japan's Economic Expansion*. London: Oxford University Press, 1965.

Beardsley, R. K., J. W. Hall, and R. E. Ward, *Village Japan*. Chicago: University of Chicago Press, 1959.

Beasley, W. G., *The Modern History of Japan*. New York: Praeger, 1963.

Beckmann, George M., *The Making of the Meiji Constitution*. Lawrence, Kan.: University of Kansas Press, 1957.

Benedict, Ruth, *The Chrysanthemum and the Sword*. Boston: Houghton Mifflin, 1946.

Butow, Robert J. C., *Japan's Decision to Surrender*. Stanford, Calif.: Stanford University Press, 1954.

———, *Tojo and the Coming of the War*. Princeton, N.J.: Princeton University Press, 1961.

Dore, R. P., *City Life in Japan*. Berkeley, Calif.: University of California Press, 1958.

———, *Land Reform in Japan*. London: Oxford University Press, 1959.

Hall, John W., and Richard K. Beardsley, *Twelve Doors to Japan*. New York: McGraw-Hill, 1965.

Hunsberger, Warren, *Japan and the United States in World Trade*. New York: Harper, 1964.

Ike, Nobutaka, *The Beginnings of Political Democracy in Japan*. Baltimore, Md.: The Johns Hopkins University Press, 1950.

Jansen, Marius B., *Changing Japanese Attitudes towards Modernization*. Princeton, N.J.: Princeton University Press, 1965.

Kawai, Kazuo, *Japan's American Interlude*. Chicago: University of Chicago Press, 1960.

Levine, Solomon B., *Industrial Relations in Postwar Japan*. Urbana, Ill.: University of Illinois Press, 1958.

Lockwood, W. W., *The Economic Development of Japan, 1868–1938*. Princeton, N.J.: Princeton University Press, 1954.

————, *The State and Economic Enterprise in Japan*. Princeton, N.J.: Princeton University Press, 1965.

Maki, John M., *Court and Constitution in Japan*. Seattle, Wash.: University of Washington Press, 1964.

Maruyama, Masao, *Thought and Behavior in Modern Japanese Politics*. London: Oxford University Press, 1963.

McLaren, W. W., *A Political History of Japan During the Meiji Era, 1867–1912*. London: Scribners, 1916.

Maxon, Y. C., *Control of Japan's Foreign Policy, 1930–1945*. Berkeley, Calif.: University of California Press, 1957.

Miller, Frank O., *Minobe Tatsukichi: Interpreter of Constitutionalism in Japan*. Berkeley, Calif.: University of California Press, 1965.

Morris, Ivan, *Nationalism and the Right Wing in Japan*. London: Oxford University Press, 1960.

Olson, Lawrence, *Dimensions of Japan*. New York: American Universities Field Staff, 1963.

Passin, Herbert, *The United States and Japan*. Englewood Cliffs, N.J.: Prentice-Hall, 1966.

Quigley, Harold S., *Japanese Government and Politics*. New York: Appleton-Century-Crofts, 1932.

Reischauer, E. O., *The United States and Japan*, rev. ed. Cambridge, Mass.: Harvard University Press, 1964.

Reischauer, R. K., *Japan: Government-Politics*. New York: Nelson, 1939.

Scalapino, Robert A., *Democracy and the Party Movement in Prewar Japan*. Berkeley, Calif.: University of California Press, 1953.

————, and J. Masumi, *Parties and Politics in Contemporary Japan*. Berkeley, Calif.: University of California Press, 1962.

SCAP Government Section, *Political Reorientation of Japan*, 2 vols. Washington, D.C.: Government Printing Office, 1950.

Steiner, Kurt, *Local Government in Japan*. Stanford, Calif.: Stanford University Press, 1965.

Storry, Richard, *The Double Patriots*. Boston: Houghton Mifflin, 1957.

Tsunoda, R., W. T. De Bary, and D. Keene, *Sources of the Japanese Tradition*. New York: Columbia University Press, 1958.

Vogel, Ezra F., *Japan's New Middle Class*. Berkeley, Calif.: University of California Press, 1963.

von Mehren, Arthur T., *Law in Japan*. Cambridge, Mass.: Harvard University Press, 1963.

Ward, Robert E., and Dankwart A. Rustow, *Political Modernization in Japan and Turkey*. Princeton, N.J.: Princeton University Press, 1964.

Yoshida, Shigeru, *The Yoshida Memoirs*. Boston: Houghton Mifflin, 1962.

APPENDIX

TABLE 1

COMPARATIVE TABLE OF NATIONAL POPULATIONS AND AREAS

Country or area	Year of census or estimate	Population	Estimated annual percentage of population increase 1958–1963	PERCENTAGE DISTRIBUTION OF URBAN AND RURAL POPULATION		
				Year	Urban population	Rural population
Asia						
Japan	1965	98,281,955	0.9%	1960	63.5%	36.5%
Chinese People's Republic	1961	686,400,000	. . .	. . . .	. . .	. . .
India	1961	435,511,606	2.3	1961	18.0	82.0
Pakistan	1961	93,831,982	2.1	1961	13.1	86.9
Burma	1965	24,732,000	2.0	. . . .	. . .	. . .
Cambodia	1964	6,230,000	2.7	1958	12.8	87.2
Indonesia	1964	102,200,000	2.2	1960	14.8	85.2
W. Irian	1964	800,000	2.3			
Laos	1965	2,500,000	2.3	. . . .	. . .	. . .
Malaysia	1964	9,137,000	. . .	1957	42.7	57.3
Malaya	1964	7,810,000	3.1			
Sabah	1964	507,000	2.8			
Sarawak	1964	820,000	2.4			
Philippines	1964	31,900,000	3.3	1956	35.3	64.7
Singapore	1965	1,884,000	3.1	1957	63.1	36.9
Thailand	1965	30,000,000	3.0	1960	11.8	88.2
No. Vietnam	1965	17,600,000	3.4		. . .	. . .
So. Vietnam	1965	16,000,000	3.3		. . .	. . .
Afghanistan	1963	14,900,000	2.8		. . .	. . .
Iran	1956	18,954,704	2.4	1956	31.4	68.6
Iraq	1957	6,339,960	1.6	1957	39.2	60.8
Israel	1961	2,183,332	3.5	1961	77.9	22.1
Jordan	1961	1,706,226	2.9	1961	47.4	52.6
Lebanon	1963	2,200,000	3.0		. . .	. . .
Saudi Arabia	1960	6,600,000	1.9		. . .	. . .
Syria	1960	4,565,121	4.2		. . .	. . .
Turkey	1960	27,754,820	2.9	1955	28.8	71.2
Yemen	1963	5,000,000	2.6		. . .	. . .
U.S.	1960	179,323,175	1.6	1960	69.9	30.1
Europe						
France	1962	46,520,271	1.3			
West Germany	1961	53,977,418	1.3			
Great Britain	1961	52,709,354	0.7	1961	80.0	20.0
U.S.S.R.	1959	208,826,650	1.7	1959	47.9	52.1

TABLE I

COMPARATIVE TABLE OF NATIONAL POPULATIONS AND AREAS (cont.)

Country or area	Total area (sq. km.)	Inhabitants per sq. km.	Year	Arable area as percentage of total area	Inhabitants per sq. km. of arable area	Period	EXPECTATION OF LIFE AT AGE 0 Male	Female
Asia								
Japan	369,661	254	1963	16.4%	1,621	1964	67.7	72.9
Chinese People's Republic	9,561,000	72	1954	11.2	641		....	....
India	3,046,232	151	1961	49.7	287	1951–60	41.89	40.55
Pakistan	946,719	104	1958	26.9	368		....	....
Burma	678,033	36	1962	21.8	165	1954	40.8	43.8
Cambodia	181,035	34	1963	16.2	210	1958–59	44.2	43.3
Indonesia	1,491,564	69	1954	11.9	580		....	....
W. Irian	412,781	2	1950	...	......			
Laos	236,800	11	1962	4.2	262		....	....
Malaysia	332,632	27	....	16.4	168	1956–58	55.78	58.19
Malaya	131,312	59	1963	18.9	312			
Sabah	76,115	7	1963	...	......			
Sarawak	125,205	7	1962	23.6	29.6			
Philippines	300,000	106	1963	37.4	284	1946–49	48.81	53.36
Singapore	581	3,250	1963	22.4	14,500			
Thailand	514,000	58	1962	19.6	296	1947–48	48.69	51.90
No. Vietnam	158,750	111	1963	19.7	564			
So. Vietnam	170,806	94	1962	18.2	117			
Afghanistan	657,500	23	1954	13.7	165		....	....
Iran	1,648,000	13	1960	10.2	113		....	....
Iraq	448,742	15	1963	25.8	55		....	....
Israel	20,700	115	1963	19.4	563		....	....
Jordan	90,185	20	1963	12.5	151	1963	70.88[1]	73.01[1]
Lebanon	10,400	212	1963	25.9	817		....	....
Saudi Arabia	2,253,300	3	1963	0.2	1,464		....	....
Syria	185,180	28	1963	48.1	51		....	....
Turkey	780,576	37	1963	33.5	106	1950–51	46.00	50.41
Yemen	195,000	26	1963	...	......		....	....
U.S.	9,363,389	20	1959	19.8	97	1963	66.6	73.4
Europe								
France	547,026	87	1963	38.8	219	1963	67.2	74.1
West Germany	247,973	224	1963	34.2	636	1960–62	66.86	72.39
Great Britain	244,030	221	1963	30.2	715	1961–63	68.0	73.9
U.S.S.R.	22,402,200	10	1956	10.3	91	1960	70	70

Source: United Nations, *Statistical Yearbook, 1964;* F.A.O., *Production Yearbook, 1964;* United Nations, *Demographic Yearbook, 1962, 1963,* and *1964;* Japan, Prime Minister's Office, *Kokusai Tōkei Yoran, 1963; 1965 Population Census of Japan: Preliminary Count;* and Mallory, Walter H., ed., *Political Handbook and Atlas of the World, 1966.*

[1] Jewish population only.

TABLE II

COMPARATIVE TABLE OF INDEXES OF INDUSTRIALIZATION *

DISTRIBUTION OF LABOR FORCE

Country or area	Year	Percent-age primary industry[1]	Percent-age second-ary industry[2]	Percent-age tertiary industry[3]	Un-classi-fied, unem-ployed, and/or others	Per capita energy con-sump-tion (1963, kg.)	Year	Total production electric energy (million KWH)
Asia								
Japan	1963	28.9%	30.5%	39.7%	0.9%	1,532	1963	160,203
Chinese People's Republic		...	...	...	...	....	1960	58,500
India	1961	72.8	11.0	15.2	1.0	170	1962	26,227
Pakistan	1961	74.9	9.3	14.8	1.0	83	1963	2,882
Burma		...	...	...	...	55	1963	522
Cambodia		...	...	...	...	48	1962	79
Indonesia	1961	71.9	8.0	18.7	1.4	111	1962	1,335
Laos		...	...	...	...	38	1960	12.8
Federation of Malaysia	1957	61.7	11.1	25.0	2.2	285[4]	1963	1,622[4]
Singapore	1957	8.3	19.0	70.1	2.6	821	1963	823
Philippine Republic	1962	57.4	12.9	22.8	6.9	191	1963	4,217
Thailand	1960	81.9	4.1	11.7	2.3	84	1962	775
South Vietnam		...	...	...	...	62	1963	398
Afghanistan		...	...	...	...	20	1963	180
Iran	1956	54.8	19.3	20.3	5.6	352	1959	907
Iraq	1957	47.7	14.2	24.8	13.3	602	1963	1,063
Israel	1963	14.7	34.6	49.9	1.4	1,473	1963	3,153
Jordan		...	...	...	...	259	1963	114
Lebanon		...	...	...	...	645	1962	551
Saudi Arabia		...	...	...	...	280		......
Syria	1963	53.9	18.2	27.2	0.7	234	1963	525
Turkey	1960	74.9	9.6	10.3	5.2	298	1963	3,965
Yemen		...	...	...	...	7		......
U.S.	1962	7.3	32.2	55.9	4.6	8,507	1963	1,011,215
Europe								
France	1962	19.8	36.7	39.5	4.0	2,788	1963	88,245
West Germany	1963	11.7	47.7	40.0	0.6	4,121	1963	147,271
Great Britain	1951	5.1	47.4	47.0	0.5	5,090	1963	173,609
U.S.S.R.	1959	38.8	36.7	19.8	4.7	3,234	1963	412,418

* Compiled from I.L.O., *Yearbook of Labor Statistics, 1964;* United Nations, *Statistical Yearbook, 1964.*
1 Agriculture, hunting, fishing, forestry. 2 Mining, manufacturing, construction. 3 Trade, utilities, finance, communications, etc. 4 Excludng Sabah and Sarawak, the figures for which are 211 and 681, respectively, for energy consumption and 29 and 32 for electric energy production. 5 Malaya only. 6 Including service traffic. 7 Excluding Sabah and Sarawak. Sabah's figures are 22 and 5, respectively.

TABLE II

COMPARATIVE TABLE OF INDEXES OF INDUSTRIALIZATION (cont.)

Country or area	Crude steel production (1963, 1,000 metric tons)	Crude steel consumption (1963, kg. per capita)	Cement production (1963, 1,000 metric tons)	Year	Volume of railway traffic (millions of: A—passenger km.; B—net ton km.)	
					A	B
Asia						
Japan	31,501	258	29,948	1963	221,411	58,100
Chinese People's Republic	12,000	16	9,000	1959	45,670	265,260
India	5,971	16	9,355	1963	88,000	92,000
Pakistan	12	7.5	1,498	1963	13,266	9,643
Burma	....	..	124	1963	1,541	734 [6]
Cambodia	....	..	....	1963	81	68
Indonesia	....	2.3	511	1963	6,262	951
Laos	....	..	....		....	....
Federation of Malaysia	....	33 [5]	362 [5]	1963	536 [7]	618 [7]
Singapore	....	..	....	1963		
Philippine Republic	....	20	951	1963	1,068	192
Thailand	....	13	998	1963	2,714	1,340
South Vietnam	....	4.7	....	1963	230	182
Afghanistan	....	..	103		....	....
Iran	....	21	745	1963	1,440	1,447
Iraq	....	25	942	1962	530	722
Israel	....	189	1,022	1963	412	317
Jordan	....	..	285		....	....
Lebanon	....	120	896	1963	5	43
Saudi Arabia	....	18	....		....	....
Syria	....	20	685	1963	57	88
Turkey	331	27	2,681	1963	3,631	3,748
Yemen	....	..	....		....	....
U.S.	99,120	540	61,609	1963	29,803	912,733
Europe						
France	17,557	326	18,060	1963	36,630	62,990
West Germany	31,597	473	29,217	1963	37,736	59,488
Great Britain	22,881	368	14,059	1963	31,503	27,041
U.S.S.R.	80,198	344	61,018	1963	192,000	1,749,400

TABLE III

COMPARATIVE TABLE OF EDUCATIONAL ATTAINMENT AND CIRCULATION OF MASS MEDIA

SCHOOL ENROLLMENT RATIOS IN 1960

Country or area	PERCENTAGE OF LITERACY [1] Year of census or survey	Percentage of total population	Unadjusted school enrollment ratios [4] Primary 5–14 years	Secondary 15–19 years	Total 5–19 years	Adjusted school enrollment ratio (primary and secondary levels)
Asia						
Japan	1960	97.8%	62%	95%	73%	91%
Chinese People's Republic		...	58	17	46	58
India	1961	23.7	32	22	29	31
Pakistan	1961	18.8	22	16	20	26
Burma	1954	57.7	31	13	26	43
Cambodia	1958	30.8	44	5	33	41
Indonesia	1961	42.9 [2]	40	13	32	40
Laos		...	20	2	15	17
Federation of Malaysia	1957	47.0 [3]	58	26	50	62
Singapore	1957	49.8	66	47	61	77
Philippine Republic	1960	71.9	56	25	47	70
Thailand	1960	67.7	59	13	46	58
South Vietnam		...	50	15	37	47
Afghanistan		...	5	1	4	5
Iran	1956	12.8	28	14	24	30
Iraq	1957	17.3	43	21	37	50
Israel	1961	84.2	83	45	74	92
Jordan	1961	32.4	51	35	46	58
Lebanon		...	64	28	53	66
Saudi Arabia		...	6	2	5	6
Syria	1960	35.4	43	20	36	45
Turkey	1960	38.1	42	17	35	47
Yemen		...	8	0.4	6	8
U.S.	1959	97.8	83	76	81	102
Europe						
France	1946	97.0	74	83	76	88
West Germany	1950	98.5	69	78	72	78
Great Britain	1950	98.5	62	107	76	81
U.S.S.R.	1959	98.5	71	27	57	78

Source: United Nations, *Statistical Yearbook, 1964;* UNESCO, *Statistical Yearbook, 1963.*

[1] Literacy is defined as the ability to both read and write. Percentages are the literate population 15 years of age and over, per 100 total population of corresponding age group.

[2] Excluding West Irian.

[3] Excluding Sabah and Sarawak, the 1960 figures for which were 23.5 and 21.5 per cent respectively.

[4] Unadjusted school enrollment ratios represent percentages of enrollment related to the

TABLE III

COMPARATIVE TABLE OF EDUCATIONAL ATTAINMENT AND CIRCULATION OF MASS MEDIA (cont.)

Country or area	Year	Daily general-interest newspaper circulation per 1,000 inhabitants	Year	Number of domestic letters sent and received (thousands)	Year	Number of radio sets (in thousands)	Number of television sets as of end of 1963 (in thousands)
Asia							
Japan	1962	420	1963	8,490,000	1963	19,318	15,153
Chinese People's Republic	1955	19	..	....	1963	8,000	50
India	1962	0.3	1963	4,697,000 c	1962	3,072	0.5
Pakistan	1962	5	1963	684,885	1962	396	....
Burma	1962	9	1963	12,582	1963	203	....
Cambodia	1962	8	..	....		....	1
Indonesia	1959	11 a	1963	200,111	1961	1,250	10
Laos	1962	11	..	....	1962	22	....
Federation of Malaysia	1960	67 b	1963	114,056 d	1962	338 e	....
Singapore	1963	283	1962	33,360	1961	149	31
Philippine Republic	1962	18	..	....	1963	1,220	70
Thailand	1960	11	1963	50,977		....	....
South Vietnam	1962	38	1963	44,213	1961	125	....
Afghanistan	1962	4	..	....	1963	25	....
Iran	1961	15	1956	125,135	1963	1,600	100
Iraq	1963	12	1953	16,825	1962	100	50
Israel	1962	148	1963	157,716	1962	539	....
Jordan	1962	27	1963	5,398	1962	63	....
Lebanon	1959	97	1963	17,099	1959	....	100
Saudi Arabia	1962	2	..	....		....	19
Syria	1962	9	..	....		....	1.5
Turkey	1961	45	1963	279,185	1963	1,633	1.5
Yemen	..	..		....		....	....
U.S.	1963	311	1963	67,853,000	1962	184,000	61,850
Europe							
France	1961	257	1963	8,179,000	1963	14,551	4,400
West Germany	1963	315	1963	8,208,000	1963	17,099	8,539
Great Britain	1962	490	1963	10,473,000	1963	15,882	12,789
U.S.S.R.	1961	181	1962	4,239,000	1962	66,000	10,000

population of the relevant age groups, i.e., 5–14 years inclusive for the primary level, 15–19 years inclusive for the secondary, and 5–19 years inclusive for the total column. Since the age levels of pupils actually enrolled in a given country do not exactly correspond to these arbitrary age groups and since the length of schooling varies widely from one country to another, the respective school enrollment ratios must be interpreted in the light of actual age ranges and the duration of primary and secondary schooling in each country. This accounts for the fact that ratios for some countries exceed 100 and that ratios at the secondary level occasionally exceed those at the primary level. The adjusted school enrollment ratios attempt to compensate for such variations by relating total enrollment, not to the arbitrary age group of 5–19 years, but to the population more nearly corresponding to the actual duration of schooling in each country.

a Excluding West Irian.

b Excluding Sabah and Sarawak, the figures for which are 37 and 25, respectively.

c Domestic and foreign mail.

d Excluding Sabah and Sarawak, the 1962 figures for which were 4,143 and 1,259, respectively.

e Excluding Sabah and Sarawak.

TABLE IV

COMPARATIVE TABLE OF GROSS, AND PER CAPITA NATIONAL PRODUCTS, 1960 *

Country or area	"MONEY" GNP Billions of dollars	"MONEY" GNP Percentage of world total	"REAL" GNP Billions of dollars	"REAL" GNP Percentage of world total	GNP PER CAPITA IN DOLLARS "Money" GNP	GNP PER CAPITA IN DOLLARS "Real" GNP (1961)
Asia						
Japan	36.0	2.6%	58.0	3.3%	383.0	613.0
Chinese People's Republic	58.0	4.2	116.0	6.6	83.0	167.0
India	29.6	2.1	59.2	3.4	69.9	139.8
Pakistan	5.6	0.4	11.2	0.6	62.4	124.8
Burma	1.3	0.1	2.6	0.1	60.6	121.2
Cambodia	0.4	.. [1]	0.8	.. [1]	77.4	154.8
Indonesia	9.2	0.7	13.7	0.8	98.6	147.9
Laos	0.1	.. [1]	0.2	.. [1]	52.0	104.0
Federation of Malaya	2.6	0.2	3.9	0.2	368.3	552.4
Philippine Republic	4.8	0.3	7.2	0.4	188.2	282.3
Thailand	2.3	0.2	4.6	0.3	101.2	202.4
South Vietnam	1.5	0.1	2.9	0.2	110.7	210.3
Afghanistan	0.8	0.1	1.5	0.1	58.5	117.0
Iran	2.5	0.2	3.8	0.2	120.3	180.4
Iraq	1.1	0.1	1.6	0.1	160.9	225.3
Israel	1.7	0.1	2.4	0.1	733.4	1,026.8
Jordan	0.2	.. [1]	0.3	.. [1]	126.3	189.4
Lebanon	0.5	.. [1]	0.8	.. [1]	319.5	479.2
Saudi Arabia	1.2	0.1	1.7	0.1	169.8	254.7
Syria	0.8	0.1	1.2	0.1	173.3	259.9
Turkey	6.3	0.5	9.4	0.5	222.5	333.7
Yemen	0.2	.. [1]	0.5	.. [1]	80.2	160.4
U.S.	515.0	37.3	515.0	29.4	2,790.0	2,790.0
Europe						
France	55.3	4.0	66.4	3.8	1,200.0	1,440.0
West Germany	65.7	4.7	89.5	5.0	1,170.0	1,590.0
Great Britain	70.4	5.1	91.5	5.2	1,340.0	1,740.0
U.S.S.R.	176.0	12.7	212.0	12.1	818.0	986.0

* Compiled with the assistance of Professor P. N. Rosenstein-Rodan and based on M. F. Millikan and D. L. M. Blackmer (eds.), *The Emerging Nations* (Boston, 1961), pp. 150–151; and P. N. Rosenstein-Rodan, "International Aid for Underdeveloped Countries," *Review of Economics and Statistics* (May, 1961), pp. 126–127.

[1] Less than 0.05 per cent.

TABLE V

COMPARATIVE TABLE OF INDUSTRIAL ORIGIN OF GROSS DOMESTIC PRODUCT AT FACTORY COST

Country or area	Year	PERCENTAGE DISTRIBUTION			Year	Gross domestic product expressed in millions of U.S. dollars	Per capita gross domestic product (U.S. dollars)
		Primary industry [1]	Secondary industry [2]	Tertiary industry [3]			
Asia							
Japan	1963	13%	39%	48%	1963	56,506	589
Chinese People's Republic	1956	48	32	20		....	....
India	1962	45	20 [4]	35 [4]	1962	34,283	76
Pakistan	1962	52	13	35	1962	7,446	77
Burma	1963	33	20	47	1963	1,493	64
Cambodia	1962	42	14	44	1963	660	115
Indonesia	1959	56	10 [5]	34 [5]	1958	6,171	69
Laos	..	..	..	..	1958	137	80
Federation of Malaysia [6]	1962	36	19	45	1962	1,794	243
Singapore	..	..	..	..	1958	571	377
Philippine Republic	1963	34	25	41	1958	4,935	191
Thailand	1963	34	19	47	1963	2,904	101
South Vietnam	..	..	..	..	1962	1,418	95
Afghanistan	..	..	..	..	1958	684	53
Iran	..	..	..	..	1958	3,316	169
Iraq	1963	16	50	44	1963	1,850	270
Israel	1963	11	32	57	1963	2,283	961
Jordan	1963	19	13	78	1963	323	177
Lebanon	1961	17	17	66	1963	437	218
Saudi Arabia	..	..	..	..	1958	1,187	195
Syria	1962	36	18	46	1963	943	175
Turkey	1963	40	22	38	1963	6,950	230
Yemen	..	..	..	..	1958	220	50
U.S.	1963	4	35	61	1963	528,287	2,790
Europe							
France	1963	9	46	47 [7]	1963	67,291	1,406
West Germany	1963	5	53	42	1963	78,480	1,416
Great Britain	1963	4	45	53 [7]	1963	73,245	1,361
U.S.S.R.	1963	20	63 [8]	17 [8]		....	....

Source: United Nations, *Yearbook of National Accounts Statistics, 1964.*
[1] Agriculture, forestry, and fishing. [2] Mining, manufacturing, and construction. [3] Utilities, transportation, communications, trade, finance, public administration, defense, etc. [4] Utilities are included in the secondary category. [5] Construction is included in the tertiary category. [6] Malaya only. [7] The sum of the primary, secondary, and tertiary figures adds to more than one hundred per cent because bank service charges imputed to enterprises have been included in tertiary industries but not deducted from the corresponding industry groups. [8] Utilities are included in the secondary category.

TABLE VI

COMPARATIVE TABLE OF EXPORTS AND IMPORTS AS A PERCENTAGE OF GROSS NATIONAL PRODUCT

Country or area	Year	Exports	Imports
Asia			
Japan	1963	10.7%	11.5%
Chinese People's Republic	..	..	
India	1962	(5.4)[1]	(7.7)[1]
Pakistan	..	..	..
Burma	1963	16.5	16.1
Cambodia	..	..	..
Indonesia	..	..	..
Laos	..	..	..
Federation of Malaysia	1962	45.0[2]	41.8[2]
Singapore	..	..	..
Philippine Republic	1963	24.5	23.3
Thailand	1963	16.1	19.4
South Vietnam	1962	5.6	18.7
Afghanistan	..	..	..
Iran	1961	23.1	16.8
Iraq	1963	49.6	25.5
Israel	1963	23.4	44.7
Jordan	1963	15.0	45.2
Lebanon	..	..	..
Saudi Arabia	..	..	..
Syria	..	..	..
Turkey	..	..	..
Yemen	..	..	..
U.S.	1963	4.6	4.3
Europe			
France	1963	13.7	13.5
West Germany	1963	19.3	17.8
Great Britain	1963	19.3	19.7
U.S.S.R.	..	..	..

Source: United Nations, *Yearbook of National Account Statistics, 1964.*
[1] ( ) indicates percentage of national income rather than of gross national product.
[2] Malaya only.

INDEX